Touching God

Also by Jon Korkidakis

*The Trojan Horse of Leadership:
Battling the Enemy We All Face* (2014)

Touching God

Discovering Prayer that Moves the Heart of God

Jon Korkidakis

Foreword by David Barker

RESOURCE *Publications* · Eugene, Oregon

TOUCHING GOD
Discovering Prayer that Moves the Heart of God

Copyright © 2021 Jon Korkidakis. All rights reserved. Except for brief quotations in critical publications or reviews, no part of this book may be reproduced in any manner without prior written permission from the publisher. Write: Permissions, Wipf and Stock Publishers, 199 W. 8th Ave., Suite 3, Eugene, OR 97401.

Resource Publications
An Imprint of Wipf and Stock Publishers
199 W. 8th Ave., Suite 3
Eugene, OR 97401

www.wipfandstock.com

PAPERBACK ISBN: 978-1-6667-1511-8
HARDCOVER ISBN: 978-1-6667-1512-5
EBOOK ISBN: 978-1-6667-1513-2

November 16, 2021 8:52 AM

Unless otherwise indicated, all Scripture quotations are taken from the Holy Bible, New Living Translation, copyright © 1996, 2004, 2015 by Tyndale House Foundation. Used by permission of Tyndale House Publishers, Carol Stream, Illinois 60188. All rights reserved.

Scripture quotations marked MSG are taken from THE MESSAGE, copyright © 1993, 2002, 2018 by Eugene H. Peterson. Used by permission of NavPress, represented by Tyndale House Publishers. All rights reserved.

The Holy Bible, English Standard Version (ESV) is adapted from the Revised Standard Version of the Bible, copyright Division of Christian Education of the National Council of the Churches of Christ in the U.S.A. All rights reserved.

This book is dedicated to my grandsons Jude and Noah

May you grow in wisdom, stature, and knowledge of the Lord

My enduring prayer for you.

Contents

Foreword by David Barker | *ix*

Preface | *xiii*

Acknowledgments | *xvii*

Introduction | *xix*

1. Origins | 1
2. We Have All Thought It | 9
3. Heavy Waits | 18
4. Enemy at the Gate | 27
5. Other-Worldly | 36
6. Duplicate | 47
7. Alignment | 59
8. Knocking on Heaven's Door | 69
9. Communication Breakdown | 79
10. Focal Point | 89
11. Of King and Kingdom | 99

Bibliography | *111*

Foreword

As for many followers of Christ prayer for me is an ongoing important and active spiritual discipline, but at the same time often confusing and not well understood, theologically or practically. I have heard many times "prayer changes things" but I read in Scripture that God does not change. So, what changes? Does he change? Do I change? Does God in his sovereignty fit me into a plan that is already in place? I have also been taught that there is a formula to prayer, and yet the prayers of the Bible don't all seem to fit that pattern. Is there such a formula? Is it binding for all my praying? Why don't all the prayers of the Bible follow the pattern? And there are many more questions.

Two things have helped me immensely in my understanding and practice of prayer. The first is a deep dive into the study of the Psalms. As I have read, re-read, and prayed these masterpieces of the heart—cries of the saints of the past—I have learned to pray. I have learned to lament, to praise, to express gratitude, to rest on God as my rock and fortress, to confess my sin, to celebrate and honor the sacred Scriptures, to engage the pilgrimage of faith with trust and hope, and enter the throne-room of Christ, the King, with confidence and a bared heart. This understanding of prayer has brought life and vitality to the reality of prayer, and these 150 God-breathed prayers continue to serve me well in my life of faith.

Jon has studied the psalms with me, and he has picked up well this aspect of prayer in his *Touching God: Discovering Prayer that Moves the Heart of God*. He talks about the collaborative relationship with God that prayer brings and how prayer works in some of the most difficult circumstances of life. This sets the stage for the wide range of responses from "hallelujah" to "How long, O LORD" that prayer embraces. He talks about the hopeful response that prayer brings in hopeless situations. How quickly do we all launch Nehemiah's arrow prayer which I am sure included the words, "Help me, O God!" when a crisis happens, or things go awry. The psalmists knew those opening words well, and while many psalms express a cry of need and even despair, the prayer inevitably ends in a doxology of hope, "Yet I will praise you."

Jon talks about releasing our worries, fears, and anxieties to God, and coupled with that the unlimited expression and practice of prayer—time of day or mode of communication. I was taught that prayer needed to follow the ACTS formula—Adoration, Confession, Thanksgiving, Supplication. This may be loosely based on the famous "Lord's Prayer," but it was never intended to lock into concrete the pattern for all prayer. The psalms clearly show this, along with the numerous biblical prayers that Jon uses throughout his book do as well. Sometimes, while we address our prayers to God, which is an act of adoration, we are not in a place to confess our sins or give thanks for forgiveness or for the place we are in right now in life. Sometimes we simply need to cry out and reach out. We need to release our worries, fears, and anxieties to God, and in a time and mode of immediacy and even desperation, as Jon has pointed out. When I hear Jesus cry on the cross "My God, my God, why have you forsaken me?" quoting the well-known lament Psalm 22, a psalm that had been prayed by the people of God for centuries, and a prayer the Jesus would have learned and prayed in the synagogue, I hear Jesus worshipping, but in his questioning God releasing his pain and sense of abandonment to God. The rest of the psalm that he knew, and his Jewish hearers knew, makes this clear.

The second thing that has helped me in my life and practice of prayer comes from a book on preaching. Darrell W. Johnson in his book *The Glory of Preaching: Participating in God's Transformation of the World* affirms that in any development of a sermon one of the points that can never be missed is what could be called a "shift in world-view."[1] In other words, sermons need to take us into the theocentric/Christocentric worldview that is revealed in the sacred Scriptures. What is the shift in morality, ethics, relationships, spirituality, sense of mission in the world, God-awareness that this biblical text points us to? Jon has picked up on this in his thoughts on prayer. He talks about the spiritual warfare that prayer engages and that the battle belongs to God. He talks about how prayer orients us to God's purposes for our lives, and helps us align our hearts with God's heart. In other words, prayer is all about God's kingdom and our place in it as citizens of that kingdom. In Johnson's concept, it is not so much a matter of what we want, but rather a matter of what God wants. Jon has pointed us in that direction well.

In returning to the Psalms, the central theological idea of God in the Psalms is God is king. Yes, he is talked about as shepherd, warrior, judge, and overlord, but these are all functions of an ancient near eastern king. Psalms that celebrate the LORD as creator quickly move to the notion that since he is creator, he is king, consistent with the king and rule motifs of Genesis 1 and 2. Psalm 23 needs to be read as "The LORD is my shepherd(-king)," and the banquet in verse 5 is in the palace, not the wilderness. A category of the psalms is called enthronement or kingship psalms, and at the literary center of the Book of Psalms are seven psalms (Psalms 93-99) that all fit this category and celebrate God as king. This sub-collection is concluded with the well-known doxology of Psalm 100, "Shout for joy to the LORD all the earth. Worship the LORD with gladness; come before him with joyful songs." The whole Book of Psalms pivots on "the LORD reigns." Jon's emphasis on the kingdom dimension as part of the prayer rhythm of our lives is both crucial and refreshing, and desperately needed in our theology and practice of prayer.

With a pastoral heart and a winsome spirit Jon invites us into the world of prayer, a world that has been written on endlessly (thus his question, "Is another book on prayer really necessary?")

---

1. Johnson, *Glory of Preaching*, 65–71.

and takes us to important places that are not necessarily new, but perhaps forgotten. He does so by rooting his thoughts deeply in the prayers of the Bible which gives his guidance to us a spirit of authenticity and authority. We need to take his invitation seriously because there is fresh life to be ignited in our lives of prayer by hearing what he has to say, and a relationship with God through Christ that can become vital and engaging.

Jon Korkidakis has written an excellent book that deserves a wide reading. *Touching God: Discovering Prayer that Moves the Heart of God* does exactly that. He helps us touch God in a pious and worshipful way and helps us engage with God who has a heart to hear and respond to his people. It is a book that many of us will want to use for our own spiritual discipline of prayer, as well as for those whom we seek to help and guide along the way of the kingdom of our Lord Jesus Christ.

David G. Barker
Professor Emeritus of Biblical Studies
Heritage College and Seminary
Cambridge, Ontario, Canada

Preface
Unexpected

Is another book on prayer truly necessary? When considering the prospect of writing this book it caused me to pause long and hard on the question. Did I really have anything of value to add, considering the last time I did an internet search of resources on prayer it garnered 254,000,000 results?[1]

Before I articulate the reasons I feel this book will be of value, I feel the need to explain how the entire idea was birthed in the first place. I was planning my yearly preaching calendar a few years ago and had a ten-week span that I was struggling to fill. After some consultation and much prayer for guidance, the overwhelming consensus was to fill the entire ten weeks with a series on prayer.

I had yet to devote a series of that length on the topic of prayer. When the time came for the series to be presented, it was clear from the outset the series resonated deeply with our congregation. In fact, I have to admit that after twenty years in pastoral ministry and over twenty-five as a professor at a Christian college and seminary, few series have impacted me as personally as this one.

I'm not sure what made the series so impactful, except to say that the primary resource for understanding prayer came out of the Scriptures. Now that may sound somewhat obvious and even obtuse, but the insights that were gleaned framed prayer for many

---

1. Google, accessed October 26, 2020.

in a refreshing and new light. For most of us, prayer is either a spiritual exercise learned by mimicking others or is taught by a person or resource that adds their own subjective preferences to the topic.

Herein lies the challenge and value of this book. How is prayer presented in Scripture, and are there areas of departure from the way we naturally have been taught or instructed? Are there, within the pages of Scripture, legitimate answers, or even hints, regarding our greatest challenges when it comes to prayer? Is there a purpose and potential to prayer that reaches well beyond normal expectations?

That may sound high and arrogant, but please understand, it comes from someone who struggled with prayer for some time. Not because I didn't value it, but because I didn't really understand it. If you, like me, long to know what lies at the heart of prayer and why it is so necessary for a vibrant spiritual life, then I hope these pages will serve us all well.

The motivation for this book revolves around two perceived problems with prayer. For one, it is fraught with much confusion as to its intent and purpose, and secondly, that it is a tool to get from God want we want or need. This second problem is not necessarily incorrect but is certainly incomplete with respect to the biblical teaching.

This book will survey a number of biblical passages that inform us and help us to answer the problems stated above, with the hope of it fueling a more comprehensive understanding of prayer. Some of the questions the book will attempt to answer are:

- How and why did prayer originate? And what can its origins teach us about its primary intent?
- There is an unstated tension in every prayer, whether we acknowledge it or not.
- How do our expectations affect the way we see prayer answered?
- We often hear that prayer is simply talking to God, but is that really true?

Preface

- What happens in the spiritual realm when we pray, and would awareness of this dimension affect the way we pray?
- When prayers are answered, why do the answers rarely come in the ways we were hoping?
- Is there a missing element to our prayers that if adopted, make our prayers more biblically authentic?
- Are there prayers that God honors more than others?

These and many more questions will be answered as we survey the selected passages throughout the book. The final chapter will bring the lessons into a cohesive summary, while concluding the spiritual benefits of an authentic prayer life.

Acknowledgments

I want to acknowledge the many who helped to bring this book to reality. First, I want to thank my family. You enrich my life in so many ways and encourage me whenever such a project grips my attention.

Thank you to Kent and Carolyn Weber for inspiration and encouragement. Kent, you especially pressed me on a regular basis to get these thoughts on prayer into book format. Thank you for never giving up on the belief that others needed to hear what this book presents.

To Dr. David Barker I want to thank you for the many years of friendship and mentoring. Your input helped to balance the historical and theological with the applicational lessons of the book. Your wisdom, friendship, and guidance are invaluable.

To Rheba Moore-Nash, your grammatical touch, inspiration, and notes of encouragement made this book far better than I ever hoped or imagined. Thank you for believing that this book matters.

To Natalie Price, thank you for your time and expertise in polishing the final manuscript. You also served as a source of encouragement and thoughtful reflection to bring this book to its present form.

Introduction

Foggy Mornings and Guilty Thoughts

I REMEMBER FEELING UNCOMFORTABLE. The kind of discomfort one feels in a crowded room when you realize you are all alone—alone in your way of thinking. I began to scour the sea of faces for a glimpse of anyone else who was squirming in their seats, but alas, it only deepened my conviction of being the odd man out. Everyone else, at least on the surface, appeared to fully accept what was transpiring on the platform before us, which just made my uneasiness grow more intense.

On the platform stood a handful of elderly gentlemen. It was my first Pastors' Conference, and the room was packed with ministry leaders from our denomination. At the time, I was just beginning my foray into church ministry, having only left the business world a year earlier. I was a relatively new believer, and yet felt this calling upon my life to enter the ministry. As excited as I was to be at the conference, I was now beginning to wonder if I had made a grave mistake.

Before the gathered crowd were men on the platform going through the details and schedules for the coming days and what to expect. It was one announcement in particular that moved me into my state of discomfort. Each morning at seven there would be a time of prayer, and everyone was being encouraged to participate. That's when I felt the lump in my throat. Don't misunderstand the reason for my uneasiness because it wasn't prayer itself that was the problem. What jolted me was the time! Did I hear them right? Seven a.m.!

Now I don't know about you but for the better part of my life seven o'clock was considered far too early to be doing anything that involved stringing two coherent thoughts together. I'm usually throwing things at any alarm clock should it dare go off before eight. But here were these saints wanting us to get into one of the most intense spiritual exercises at a time when I could not get my own name right. It made me queasy.

At the same time, I felt wholly inadequate. How could something this simple and natural to others be so intimidating to me? My uneasiness with the early morning prayer invitation was rooted in guilt. At the time I was anything but a morning person. At best I could barely drag myself out of bed in the morning to get to the office. I had been the proverbial nighthawk for years and only in these recent months was I training my internal clock to a whole different rhythm. It was not easy shifting my natural cycles, and yet the most spiritual exercise we were invited to do together as a group was happening at a time that made me cringe.

I also knew that if I did my best and got out of bed, I would risk further embarrassment by potentially falling asleep if my eyes were shut for too long. Imagine some well-meaning minister waxing eloquent only to be interrupted by my loud snoring. At least that was the way it played out in my head.

It likely goes without saying that I never made it to any of those early morning prayer meetings. For the longest time I felt like a spiritual lightweight because I could not bring myself to those sunrise kneel-ins. I even tended to avoid those I knew were in charge of the conference, in case they asked me about my absence.

Growing Discontent

Looking back these many years later at that early experience, it's almost laughable. I have long turned the tables on late nights and early mornings. What was much harder to release over time was

Introduction

the expectation it created around prayer. This expectation was one I had not recognized until it had been entrenched much later, almost as a doctrine, at that faithful conference.

This expectation was that prayer is what we do first thing in the morning. Even though, at the time, I was far more bothered by the hour of participation, the real conflict that was seeded that day revolved around the time of day best suited for praying.

In the subsequent years that followed the conference experience, the notion of prayer as a morning first staple became reinforced on multiple occasions. Whether it came from well-meaning mentors who stressed the early morning prerogative to the biographies of prayer warriors who would collect themselves in the pre-dawn moments of the day and pray for hours on end, the die appeared to be cast.

What I was subjectively learning about prayer is that if I didn't start my day with it, or spend countless hours at it, I was doomed to failure. If I was not a quiet or contemplative type, then the predominance of what was being touted as a model for effective prayer was outside my natural bent and make-up.

What complicated my sense of futility was the inability to argue against it. You cannot say that getting up early and praying for long stretches is a bad thing. I started to feel that something was wrong with me. Because I was not wired for early morning prayer, or long focused bouts of intense praying, I believed that I would never become effective in that area of my spiritual life.

For all of its importance, I was never really taught how to pray. Most of us learn by modeling what we hear from others. I can remember as a pastoral intern being put in situations where I was expected to offer up a prayer while feeling the least prepared or qualified to do so. But as they say the best way to learn is to jump in with both feet.

So, in those moments, I would do what most of us would do, pray in the pattern of others that we heard. Quote a Scripture verse, evoke a blessing, cap it off with a little, "In Jesus' Name," and give the "Amen."

Introduction

It didn't matter the setting or group I was with, prayer appeared to be exclusively reserved for asking God to answer our requests, whatever the need. The main purpose was the spiritual version of a "to-do" list, complete with the sense of accomplishment that comes whenever a task can be checked from the list.

I can remember the countless small groups where we would sit in a circle and take prayer requests. Then, when they were exhausted, we would enter into the official time of prayer. That always confused me. Did God not hear the requests as they were being made? Does he not act on them until they are presented formally in an officially called prayer circle? It appeared so manufactured to me.

I was not trying to be difficult or even disrespectful, but if what I was witnessing was meant to be the true picture of prayer, then I wanted to find out why I was struggling so much with what I was seeing. So, as with any topic I needed to learn more about, I took to the latest resources to find out what I was missing.

To my surprise and bewilderment, most of what I read rarely helped. These resources seemed only to reinforce stereotypes or the author's particular preferences. There were a couple that probed deeper into the mechanics of prayer, but the scarcity of such resources caused me great concern and only increased the notion that I was alone in this wilderness called prayer.

Is It Just Me, Or Are We Missing Something?

There have been many studies on how people engage with God—from the sensate who connects through the senses and is more intuitive in their faith, to the extrovert who connects whenever they are serving in visible and practical ways. (I personally connect best with God on a clear night when the stars are out, and the majesty of the universe is presented in its entire splendor).

Because we all connect with God in various ways that are geared to our personality, it is often reflected in the preferences we have concerning spiritual disciplines. But here lies a warning. If we are not careful, the preferences become the prescription, not

Introduction

simply the expression. We can soon convince ourselves that the right way to pray is akin to the expression we feel most comfortable with. It even becomes nostalgic. Prayer can quickly migrate into rote statements and comfortable patterns based on what suits us best.

If there is one thing that we all want in our prayer lives, it is to better understand what constitutes authentic prayer that touches the heart of God. Not only the answers to the how and why of prayer, but actual answers to the prayers themselves. Otherwise, why bother?

The options for how God answers prayer are really quite limited. They can be summarized as follows:

1. Yes.
2. Yes, but not in the way you expected.
3. No.
4. Not now, but someday, maybe?
5. Silence.

Of the five options only the first one feels the most satisfying. After all, it best resolves the reasons why most of us bother to pray in the first place. The other four are what I believe to be the most commonly experienced answers we receive.

This is purely anecdotal, though it comes from years of observation in college and seminary environments and pastoral ministry, that prayers are rarely answered exactly in the way and manner that we expect them. We will unpack this further in a later chapter, but for now I will say that this creates a dilemma for many well-meaning believers who have used prayer as a one-sided conversation, rather than a relational one.

With that said, I want to make one note at this juncture. There is a danger to prayer. It can, if not tended to properly, become one of the most selfish things we do. If we are brutally honest with ourselves, the majority of our prayers can linger into the realm of personal needs and requests. That is a reality I've witnessed and experienced in my own prayer walk.

Introduction

The drama that becomes our life determines the priorities of our prayers. Not that this is always a bad thing, or that it's wrong when the difficulties we experience overwhelm us and bring us to our knees. But it can become the exclusive reason for bothering with prayer at all.

I call this the first dimension of prayer—the personal dimension that deals exclusively with our own needs and desires. Whenever we are faced with a personal crisis, decision, or need, these prayers are focused on how God will answer them for our personal benefit and gain. It is so immediate that by sheer emotional force alone we are drawn to it almost intuitively.

The second dimension is when prayer moves into petitioning God on behalf of others, or what can be called the community dimension (or relational dimension). Whenever we pray in this way, whether for an individual or group, we are asking for God to intervene in the lives of others.

Those are the two primary dimensions for prayer. From my experience they are what take the overwhelming majority of airtime when we pray—the personal and the community, the needs that are mine versus the petitions we invoke for others.

Those are pretty rudimentary categories, and they admittedly cover a broad range of prayer requests and expressions. Though there are many biblical examples that affirm these as legitimate reasons for prayer, there is a third dimension that I contend predominates the scriptural landscape.

I would argue that when it comes to prescriptions for prayer, this third dimension is where you will find them, while the two dimensions mentioned above are where we are given tremendous freedom. Yet, we seem to have the essential priorities reversed where our personal outweighs the biblical.

In the pages that follow, we will look at specific passages related to prayer, primarily to understand the means by which prayer can act as a catalyst for real change in our lives. After all, would we not want to experience the full benefit that prayer was meant to bring?

Introduction

Longing for More

Despite my own misgivings around the way prayer is typically practiced, there is a more disparaging reality. If prayer is as potent as we claim, why is so much of our North American culture sliding into its godless state? Considering how quickly we have seen tectonic shifts in the moral and ethical climates that were typically characterized by biblical values, why has the tide not been stemmed by a call to prayer?

Why do we at least not see it stemmed in the sense of slowing it to a crawl and not witnessing centuries of reverent tradition washed away in a decade? Do not misunderstand me, I am not advocating for a type of reconstructionist theology here, but one has to wonder that for all of our church growth and evangelism strategies why do we continue to see a growing exodus from the church? Why do the apparent victories appear small and hard won?

All pessimism aside, the current state of the spiritual climate should make all believers take notice. I have witnessed in my short lifetime, a faith that was once respected, slide into derision, and by all accounts, soon will be considered dangerous. If anything, this ought to be the reality that prompts every church to pull out the proverbial stops when it comes to prayer.

I don't have all the answers by any means, and God has his own reasons for allowing culture to migrate in the way it has. In fact, some will quote end-time prophecies to validate the present situation. However, I do believe that we are missing a vital ingredient that should and must be included in the discipline of our prayers—a component that is witnessed throughout Scripture and demonstrated by every faithful witness in its pages.

Could it possibly be, that because the predominance of our prayers is focused on our personal and relational needs that part of God's intent for praying has largely been neglected? And because of that neglect, we have lost our way to the heart of God? A heart that longs for much more than simply satisfying what concerns we have in the moment. If prayer is a two-way conversation, who is listening to whom and who is doing the majority of the talking? If prayer is meant to move mountains, then why are we still at base camp?

Let me be clear, I am not disparaging prayer that seeks to petition God for real needs that have real consequences should God not respond. That would be callous and unbiblical. What I am stating is that God intended much more. It is this added component that this book will investigate, and hopefully convince you to incorporate into your prayer life.

Within the pages that follow are passages that will help us to understand prayer in a richer way, with the intent of not only enriching our lives but every life that we come into contact with. As we will see, prayer is an incredible catalyst for change, especially when it is understood in all its fullness. And when we embrace and understand it in this way, it will elevate our prayers beyond, "help me, bless me, give me," and allow us to experience what happens when we touch the heart of God.

1

Origins

Origins are important. They help us to understand not only our individual backgrounds but our shared histories. They give us a sense of who we are, and how our lineage has shaped us into the people we are today. Our origin stories give us a sense of purpose and a confirmation that we belong to something larger than ourselves. When we understand our roots, we begin to understand who we are.

They also help answer the question of why? Why you may have a genetic disposition to certain health problems, like diabetes or heart disease. Or why your hair and eyes are the color they are. Often, to understand where we are today takes, to some degree, an understanding of where we were yesterday.

The Book of Genesis is all about origins. The origin of the universe, the origin of sin, the origin of the Abrahamic covenant, the nation of Israel, and for our purposes in this chapter, the origins of worship and prayer.

Embedded within the origin narratives of Genesis is the unfolding of the human experience, an experience that is marred by the Fall as found in chapter 3. From the pristine scenes of chapters 1 and 2 of a perfect creation, chapter 3 becomes a jarring corruption of all that God deemed good.

As sin enters the creation order the subsequent chapters demonstrate the ever-growing nature of sin into every facet of our lives. Everything is now in conflict with each other, flesh against spirit, animal against humanity, and humanity against itself.

Few stories crystallized the deep fracturing that sin has now created than the story of Cain and Abel that begins in chapter 4. Two brothers, related by blood and lineage—a bond that should have communicated safety and security was instead the fuel for conflict. What is telling is that the conflict is primarily centered on worship.

Family Feud

Cain is the older of the two brothers and becomes a "worker of the ground," while his younger brother, Abel, grows to be a "keeper of the sheep." From their respective livelihoods, each brings an offering to the Lord. It is here that a distinction is made between the two offerings, even though the same Hebrew word is used for both. It is the description of the offerings that is worth noting.

Abel brings the best of his flock. The Hebrew terminology is that Abel brought a firstborn, a subtle nod implying his attitude towards the act of coming with an offering before the Lord. In Cain's case, he simply brings "fruit from the ground". The contrast is simple, yet there is a hint that something is amiss. Abel's offering is noted favorably by God, but Cain's is not.

Remember, this story is long before the Law given at Sinai and is long before any formal instructions were given concerning offerings. An offering from a field is equally as acceptable as an offering from the flock. It is not the offering per se that is the problem, but the heart behind it.

It would be natural to see within the story the lurking questions behind God's favoritism of Abel over Cain, or even to ponder what was wrong with Cain's gift. But to do so would miss the greater lesson. The key lies in Cain's response to rejection, a hurt that festers within and cries for affirmation.

And in the case of Cain, God is aware of the seething anger that is stirring in the heart of the older sibling, evidenced by the fallenness of Cain's face, a Hebrew idiom denoting a posture of dejection. Though God approaches and even cautions Cain concerning his attitude, the story ends tragically with Cain murdering Abel and burying him to hide his crime. A heart, darkened by sin, is a difficult one to assuage.

Herein lies the crux, sin is already beginning to be felt among the created order. Cain's reaction to rejection was not a motivation to improvement or even contriteness. Cain's need to be accepted is normal, even universal, but his response to the seeming rejection was his and his alone. Hence the warning from God of what he knew of Cain. That "Sin is crouching at the door, eager to control you. But you must subdue it and be its master" (Genesis 4:7b). And control him it did, to an unspeakable act, rooted in Cain's need for acceptance, despite the seeming insufficiencies that may have been part of his original offering.

Cain was not to blame for being number two, it was his brother, Abel, who stood in the way. How dare the younger brother usurp the older! So, what do you do when someone stands in your way? Do you eliminate the competition? Rather than being a master of the sin, or at the very least, acknowledging what sin is now activating in the darkness of his soul, sin is now in control of Cain and has taken mastery over him. Any attempt to subdue the sin is never entertained. It is the natural outworking when hatred, jealousy, envy, and a host of other sin-induced emotions are allowed to run their course.

Far-Reaching Consequences

As punishment, God banishes Cain from his presence. As chapter 4 continues we are introduced to others who are born into the lineage of Cain, who clearly show the exponential rise of sin within the human condition. Another progression is also introduced at this juncture of the text. A telling fork-in-the-road moment that is continued throughout the remainder of Genesis—the exponential rise of sin and the apparent distancing of God from close proximity to humans.

What appeared in the early stages of the creation story of a God who is spatially near, now presents him as becoming physically distant. Prior to this moment, God's presence is comparable to walking with a friend. He is knowable because he is there, present, and unmistakably real. Conversation is natural and uninhibited with no hint of it being anything but part of the natural order of things.

But as sin escalates, God separates, in a way that is different from before. As predicted, the eyes of creation have been opened as well as the knowledge of good and evil. The trajectory of the Fall has been exponentially tragic. Separation from God becomes a type of exile, and the conflict that results from the Fall, a constant reminder of why the separation exists in the first place.

As the march of sin progresses, so does the human population. The chapter concludes with new arrivals in the family of Adam and Eve, including a son named Seth, who when he is of age, has a son named Enosh. Connected to these births the chapter concludes in this manner:

> To Seth also a son was born, and he called his name Enosh. At that time people began to call upon the name of the LORD (Genesis 4:26 ESV).

The last sentence of the chapter can easily be missed, or even deemed a natural progression, but it dares not be considered insignificant. It's a summary statement of sorts, giving weight to the transitions in creation that have brought us here, but it is also a harbinger of what is now a new normal. As Genesis is a book of origins, here again, we are presented with the inception of something new—worship, and the context from which it was borne.

Sin has become the great separator between God and man. What was once a relationship of closeness is now met with the barrier of distance, and more importantly, sin. We cannot walk away from this chapter without acknowledging that to call upon the Lord's name is not only a communication tool but a recognition tool. At the heart of it, and as a reality of its function, is the acknowledgment of the separation that sin has brought to the world and the necessity of calling on the Lord as the vehicle that spans the chasm.

What is in a Name?

To call upon the name of the Lord is undeniably a picture first and foremost of prayer, a significant component of worship. But here, in these early stages of the biblical story, it plays a critical part in creating an understanding of not only its origins, but also of the essential role it plays in the lives of those who seek communion with the Creator.

Some commentators see this closing sentence as a general description for worship while others denote the term, "call" as a form of proclamation. Though there is merit to their argument, they seem too generic and too nondescript for the context. There is an implied intention of purpose to the proclamation and an intention of direction as well. Both of which lend themselves to the foundational understanding of prayer that forms our modern concepts.

Prayer acknowledges that we are in need of help, for the darkness that we have been plunged into as a consequence of the Fall is real and beyond our ability to rectify. At least, not without divine help and enablement are we able to rectify it. For those who see the weight that has befallen the world, a cry is lifted up, but not to a nameless one, but to the only One.

Names in the ancient near east are important. But here, these names are not empty platitudes to an empty or unknowable God. This is the God of creation, a creation marked by his word, breath, and hands. The word for LORD here is Yahweh, the personal, intimate name of God. Early in the biblical account, we have an indication that the name that God revealed to Moses at the burning bush was acknowledged by the earliest believers, who are raising their voices in open and unhindered manner to the Lord.

The closing verse further proposes a distinction, contrasted by those who believe and those who do not. Prayer is fundamentally an act of worship, not a vehicle for transactional exchange. In other words, unlike the pagans who only appear before the gods as a last resort or when the need is great, those who call upon the name of the Lord understand this action primarily as a relational one.

To that end, let's remember what the relationship between God and Adam and Eve looked like. A common illustration for the relationship was God walking among them. As stated earlier, this is presented in the Bible as real as you and a friend walking down the street. In fact, throughout the remainder of the Bible the picture of "walking" with the Lord is a common one. It's the same relational picture that we find in the New Testament as Jesus is calling people to himself. <u>To walk with the Lord is to be in close, personal fellowship with him</u>.

Walking with the Lord

Has prayer, or calling upon the name of the Lord, in the context of Genesis, now become another form of once again walking in close fellowship with the Lord? What other tool is there to span the distance, however seemingly arbitrary or metaphysical it is? The act of calling upon the name of the Lord enters the human experience just as the exponential rise of sin creates a separation from God.

There is another implied expectation in this verse, one which is carried forward from the entirety of chapter 4. As the world continues with many following in the footsteps of Cain, the separation between God and humanity will continue to grow over time. As the years progress and the memories of the early creation period wane, so too are the lessons of that history. There will always be those who generation after generation, acknowledge the true place of the Lord in their lives. However, for many, the vacuum created by the separation and fading memory will no doubt have an impact.

Waning memories have a way of creating doubt and even suspicion of the original narrative, and over time, new gods, new philosophies, new world views, and new creation narratives, will begin to appear. This is a byproduct of a humanity that refuses to acknowledge a Creator, therefore creating alternate narratives of their own invention and convention. But here, in these early, unfiltered stages, when all is raw, there is the recognition for those who see clearly that there is only one narrative that matters, one rooted in the Lord.

Prayer also reminds us that there is more than just what we see around us. Cain's view was too narrow and limiting. It was too focused on the self—my need, my hurt, my rejection. When our worldview shrinks so does our faith. The more our narcissism takes over, the more we pine for our wants as opposed to seeking what the Lord can provide. And when our wants are unmet, from the framework of our own limited and narcissistic understanding, we tend to distort even the best that life has to offer, such as love, justice, and mercy.

This juncture in Genesis also denotes an opposite decision—the conviction to rely on our own selves to make it in the world, that we are the agents of our own destinies and outcomes. God is no more than periphery to our own devices, instincts, and will, and dare not interfere with the destiny we have envisioned for ourselves. There is the abject refusal to acknowledge that a basic element of a person's life is their turning towards God.

Eugene Peterson writes that, "a life of prayer is the result of an understanding and decision—an understanding that God is personally involved in everything that's going on in me and in the world, and a decision that I want to participate in it on his terms."[1]

Prayer ultimately becomes this doorway to seeing the world and ourselves through God's eyes, and in doing so, demands a transformation of the heart. The world is not as God intended. We live in a fallen world. We live in a broken world. We live in a world that needs to be healed. Yet, in the midst of the fallenness, God did not leave us without hope.

As a final thought, it would be remiss to neglect what this also teaches us about God himself. For sin to enter the world took a conscious and deliberate act of disobedience. Yet, as destructive and defiant as that was, God still made a way for us to commune and walk with him. For those who see the darkness that sin has

---

1. Peterson, *The Message Bible*, 1841.

brought upon the world, prayer becomes the vehicle for hope and healing, but most of all, for walking intimately with the Lord.

We can mistakenly assume that God's primary desire is to serve him. This is not a bad assumption to make, but it does divert our attention from the primary one—to be with God. We can treat prayer as a vehicle for a help me, bless me, give me mentality, but God is seeking a transformed heart that says, be with me, walk with me, talk with me. We can often be overwhelmed by the circumstances of life that we experience as a result of the Fall, but we are never left alone. In the following pages we will hopefully deepen our appreciation and understanding of prayer as it was originally intended, as a vehicle for walking with God, in the intimate portrayal as presented in the early pre-Fall conditions of Genesis.

2

We Have All Thought It

Few moments prompt us to pray like a crisis. Nothing drives us to our knees faster than those moments that tear our lives apart. They flood us with feelings of helplessness, uncertainty, pain, and emotional upheaval. They remind us how quickly life can feel beyond our control and ability to fix; and in those moments, divine help is often where we turn.

If there is ever a time we have wanted our prayers answered it's in a crisis. The prayers that seek the reversal of a terminal diagnosis, protection as a category five storm approaches, or the safe return of a child who has been abducted are all prayed fervently. The scenarios of a crisis are many, but despite the variety, the answers are almost always the same. They are answers that seek a reversal or respite from whatever storm or tragedy we are experiencing. As a pastor, I have asked people many times how I could be praying for them. In crisis moments, I've rarely had to ask. Not only do I know the specifics of what the prayer would entail, but also the answer the individual is longing to receive.

It is here where one of the greatest tensions concerning prayer arises. It is rarely spoken aloud, but the tension is there, nonetheless. It's the question lurking in the background, which in many ways, challenges our faith and what we truly believe.

The Tension is Real

To help illustrate this tension we are going to look at an amazing story from the Old Testament found in 2 Chronicles chapter 20. It's about a king named Jehoshaphat who faced a crisis, one that could potentially bring ruin to the nation of Judah. Jehoshaphat has just received news that three armies—the Moabites, Ammonites, and Edomites—are amassing to attack. In fact, this vast army is practically on the doorstep and within striking distance. The news terrifies the king, and he takes immediate action.

What would one expect of a king who faces such a crisis? I am sure it would seem incredibly natural for Jehoshaphat to call together his generals for a strategic battle plan or immediately order the reinforcement of the city walls. We would not find it unnatural if he would call up every able-bodied person for military service. Maybe call for all women and children to Helm's Deep. Okay, I couldn't resist that last one.

But he doesn't do any of that . . . instead, he begins to pray and orders the entire nation to begin fasting. As enemies are amassing on their borders, people from all over Judah come to Jerusalem to seek the Lord's help. The reaction to the threat is one of petition first and foremost. For Jehoshaphat, any battle plan determined without first seeking the Lord is likely doomed from the start.

Here is the prayer that Jehoshaphat offers beginning in verse 5:

> [5] Jehoshaphat stood before the community of Judah and Jerusalem in front of the new courtyard at the Temple of the LORD. [6] He prayed, "O LORD, God of our ancestors, you alone are the God who is in heaven. You are ruler of all the kingdoms of the earth. You are powerful and mighty; no one can stand against you! [7] O our God, did you not drive out those who lived in this land when your people Israel arrived? And did you not give this land forever to the descendants of your friend Abraham? [8] Your people settled here and built this Temple to honor your name. [9] They said, 'Whenever we are faced with any calamity such as war, plague, or famine, we can come to

stand in your presence before this Temple where your name is honored. We can cry out to you to save us, and you will hear us and rescue us.' [10] "And now see what the armies of Ammon, Moab, and Mount Seir are doing. You would not let our ancestors invade those nations when Israel left Egypt, so they went around them and did not destroy them. [11] Now see how they reward us! For they have come to throw us out of your land, which you gave us as an inheritance. (2 Chronicles 20:5–11)

Jehoshaphat's prayer up to this point is in many ways a theological treatise on the nature of God and a recounting of the nation's history with him. It is also an acknowledgment that God is the only viable source of help for the crisis the nation now faces. It stresses the first tension that we often face when we pray, especially when we are seeking help for a situation beyond our ability to bring to resolution by our own strength.

The Questions that Create Tension

This first tension is the *can he* question. Can God fix this? Can God do what we are unable to do in this situation or circumstance? For Jehoshaphat and the nation of Judah, the answer is a resounding yes! The nation has seen the mighty hand of God in the past. His power has been evidenced in other moments in the nation's history and, without a doubt, this is another crisis that God can easily avert. No human weapon can match the Lord.

For anyone who has a shred of faith in God, the matter of whether or not God is powerful enough or able to fix whatever problem we are faced with is an easy one to reconcile. Of course, God can. He is God. Omnipotent, omniscient, omnipresent and a host of other theological categories that are indicative of the most powerful being in the universe. The One who spoke the universe into being by just the breath of his mouth. In fact, what kind of God would he be if he wasn't powerful?

As with the prayer of Jehoshaphat in 2 Chronicles 20, there is confident assurance in the Lord's power and ability in the face of the present crisis. This is an army and a threat that cannot be averted through human ingenuity or might. It needs divine intervention. As far as the prayer presented so far, the final verse of the prayer has been left till now. The reason is simple. In this closing verse we have what Jehoshaphat seeks as an answer from the Lord, and with it an introduction to the second tension of prayer.

> [12] O our God, won't you stop them? We are powerless against this mighty army that is about to attack us. We do not know what to do, but we are looking to you for help. (2 Chronicles 20:12)

You see, the critical question for Jehoshaphat is not whether God *can do it* – it is whether or not *he will do it*? The king, at a moment of great need, speaks a refrain that has been quoted for centuries, "We are looking to you for help." And isn't that the great point of tension for many of us when we pray? We know that God has the power, ability, and the resources to overcome anything. Nothing is beyond him. The greater tension comes as we ask ourselves, "Will God respond?"

This natural tension intrinsic to prayer is one of the great challenges for many of us. We have all experienced desperate prayers that were met with silence. Prayers that revolved around a diagnosis, a critical need, or a similar request that was never resolved. We have all experienced those moments when we desperately sought action, or at the very least an answer from God.

Nothing tests the solidity of faith like the silence of an unanswered prayer. We pleaded, asked, and even begged, but when all is said and done, the lack of divine intervention resulted in an outcome that begs the ever-present question of, "Why?" Few outcomes challenge the notions of a good God more than the emptiness of divine silence, especially when the stakes are at their highest.

I've witnessed the wrestling of one's faith in these dark moments. For some, they lean into God even more than before the ordeal, but for others, it becomes the beginnings of a faith crisis or an exit from faith in God altogether. Questions that are key to human closure and recovery are often left unanswered or murky at best. *Why did God ignore my plea? Was there something I did wrong?* The questions longing for an answer are countless. The aftermath of such an experience is devastating.

If faith is a matter of trust, it is here at this juncture where a critical decision lies in the heart of any person who has lived through such a crisis. Is God, even after this experience, worthy of being trusted? Here we have the many platitudes by well-meaning people who try to lessen the impact of your experience by spouting doctrinal formulas or spiritual aphorisms while at the same time neglecting the deep hurt and pain we are feeling.

This is not to give the impression that for the majority, God is silent in matters closest to our hearts. If anything, stories abound of prayers that have been answered in ways that can only be categorized as miraculous. Tumors that mysteriously disappear, coincidences that defy reason, relational transformations that go beyond human reckoning, and many more examples too numerous to list.

For every seemingly unanswered prayer the opposite exists as well. Miraculous interventions that defy logic yet clearly point to a divine hand. We do struggle in seasons when God does not answer, but in moments when he does, the circumstances, timing, outcome, and collateral benefits are too real and specific to explain away. Divine intervention, when it arrives, leaves little doubt of its benefactor.

For Jehoshaphat and the people of Judah, though, the tension of *will he?* comes relatively quickly. Beginning in verse 14, the plea of the king is soon answered:

> [14] the Spirit of the LORD came upon one of the men standing there. His name was Jahaziel son of Zechariah, son of Benaiah, son of Jeiel, son of Mattaniah, a Levite who was a descendant of Asaph. [15] He said, "Listen, all you people of Judah and Jerusalem! Listen, King Jehoshaphat! This is what the LORD says: Do not be afraid! Don't be discouraged by this mighty army, for the battle is not yours, but God's. [16] Tomorrow, march out against them…[17] But you will not even need to fight. Take your positions; then stand still and watch the LORD's victory.

He is with you, O people of Judah and Jerusalem. Do not be afraid or discouraged. Go out against them tomorrow, for the LORD is with you!" (2 Chronicles 20:14–17)

What is introduced in these four verses has much to teach us about prayer. In fact, it is part of a general pattern that exists throughout the Scriptures.

The Choices We Make

The first observation comes from recognizing that the Spirit of the Lord comes upon a man in the crowd. Frankly, there is no real surprise there, but what is striking is the specificity of the person who is chosen. In articulating his lineage there is a credibility factor to his pronouncement. This is someone related to the priestly line of the Levites and even a descendant of Asaph who authored a number of psalms (Assuming it is this Asaph that is being referred to).

Reading further from these verses, there is never a hint of doubt by the assembly as to the veracity of what has been revealed. His lineage and heritage serve as a kind of confirmation of the revelation being authentic. The king and the people respond by bowing down in worship and then singing with loud praises. With respect to king Jehoshaphat, there is humble deference on his part to Jahaziel, through whom the Spirit has spoken. Jehoshaphat may be king, but he exudes no pride in this moment of divine revelation.

Twice in the words spoken by Jahaziel is the Hebrew phrase, "Do not fear, do not be dismayed," (the NLT rendering of "Do not be afraid! Do not be discouraged . . . "). Even though the answer that God is giving will result in a miraculous intervention, there is still a recognition of the emotional toll that is being experienced by the people. Besides the acknowledgement by God of what is happening on a visceral level, it is also a statement that asks in no uncertain terms, "Do you trust God?"

Fear, is a highly charged emotion, and frankly, one of the most misunderstood as far as the biblical picture is concerned. The fear in this story is very real because the threat is real. If Jehoshaphat paid no mind to the enemies on his borders and acted with no concern or attempts to protect the nation it would not only have been irresponsible, it would have likely killed many of his own people.

Fear encompasses a broad range of human experiences, from the insignificant to life-threatening, which fosters an unending list of potential reasons for seeking divine help in the first place. That being said, God acknowledges the fear that the situation has provoked while at the same time presenting an option that clearly points to hope, rather than fear. Fear is often the provocation that drives us to prayer in the first place, and that is exactly the point. An upcoming chapter will deal with the place of fear further.

The recognition by God of the people's fear is a further indication of the relational component of prayer. If prayer is nothing more than a transaction between creator and created, why bother acknowledging human factors like fear in the first place? Transactional religion is rooted in a system whereby you negotiate a need by placating the particular god with whatever offering necessary.

Transactional worship is nothing more than a religious bartering system whereby I offer something in return for what I need. Biblical prayer is rooted first and foremost as a relational interaction. One of the grandest illustrations of this comes out of John's Gospel. In chapter 11, Jesus raises Lazarus from the dead. The undeniable magnitude of such a miracle cannot be minimized. Yet, prior to Jesus performing this miracle for all to witness, he pauses to weep (John 11:35). Why even bother weeping considering the outcome if Jesus couldn't care less about the emotional state of those around him?

This aspect of prayer will continue to unfold in subsequent chapters but for now, the answer given by God to the people of Judah warrants further notice. Jahaziel reminds the people that the battle is God's, and not theirs. This is so important to note. God will fight for us, because the battle is his. Sometimes we feel we have to do it all, face it all, and we can be overwhelmed by the seemingly endless barrage of battles we face every day. But, whenever we give those battles to the Lord he will fight for us because God is for us.

What is disclosed next is somewhat intriguing. As the next day dawns, the army heads out to meet the enemy but rather than face them in battle, they instead witness the Lord's victory.

Battle Ready

I've wondered what the point was in sending the army out in the first place. God could have easily rendered the defeat of the enemy forces without the added necessity of an early morning march. Imagine what the evening prior would have looked like. Was it a restless night for the soldiers anticipating what faced them in the morning? As the new day began, what was the mood of the people as their army clothed themselves in battle gear while sharpening sword and spear? In verse 20 we read the following encouragement from the king, which speaks to the potential concern he may have had about his soldiers doubting:

> [20] Early the next morning the army of Judah went out into the wilderness of Tekoa. On the way Jehoshaphat stopped and said, "Listen to me, all you people of Judah and Jerusalem! Believe in the LORD your God, and you will be able to stand firm. Believe in his prophets, and you will succeed." (2 Chronicles 20:20)

As the army of Judah went out to meet the enemy, they did so on the word of one man. Granted, the text is clear as to Jahaziel being prompted by the Spirit of God, but the revelation he gave was a miracle of substance, one that provoked either trust, or doubt. Even so, in reading the remainder of the chapter we are told Jehoshaphat placed singers ahead of his army who sang the refrain, "Give thanks to the Lord; his faithful love endures forever." It was the king's way of affirming his trust in God.

We are told that at the moment they began to sing, God caused the enemy armies to fight amongst themselves until every one of them was destroyed. When Jehoshaphat and his army came upon the scene, it was strewn with bodies as far as they could see. What they realize in that moment is a lesson not easily forgotten.

To witness the word of God spoken from one man and then the aftermath of that battle scene would have crystallized forever in their minds the importance of trusting God.

Prayer not only plays a major part in the story of Jehoshaphat and the threat the nation faces, but it also becomes the catalyst for the miracle that unfolds. Jehoshaphat, as king, could have responded to the threat in natural, human ways. Some would even say this was the most natural reaction to the fear that such a threat would impose. Instead, he calls the nation to fasting and prayer and it becomes the catalyst for God to act.

We began the chapter highlighting a common tension in prayer, the pressure of *can he?* versus, *will he?* Though the story in 2 Chronicles 20 is one where God miraculously intervened, it still illustrates the further relational tension of trusting God, regardless of whether or not the outcome is what we wanted. This is the lesson God intended by still making the army prepare itself for battle, even though it was unnecessary.

When a crisis presents itself, we are faced with a decision: Do we allow fear to reign, or do we trust God? No doubt this was the decision that presented itself when the news of an enemy army reached the ears of king Jehoshaphat. His decision to take the matter to God was the most importance decision in the entire story, because had he done otherwise, the nation may very well have fallen into enemy hands. His first reaction was to take it to God and trust the outcome to him.

3

Heavy Waits

WE LIVE IN A purpose-driven world. Whether we are talking about church or the marketplace, knowing the reason why we exist and what we were made for gives meaning to our daily struggles. Knowing our purpose, or at least being convinced that we have been made for something larger than ourselves, can motivate us to strive in situations that would leave others paralyzed. Purpose points us beyond the present into a hopeful future. It can make the challenges of the present nothing more than stepping stones to a greater and more rewarding tomorrow—because purpose infuses our lives with meaning. The gravitational pull it exerts makes it very attractive.

Before the existence of the purpose driven movement there existed another, equally moving and with equally challenging language. In simpler days it was coined with the term *"burden."* We are not talking about *being* a burden here, but *having* a burden. It's a weight we carry for a particular cause, or a mission. It's something that propels us to action in a way that does not allow us to shrug it off or put it to the back of our minds. When a burden has us in its sights, the only reasonable thing to do is surrender to it.

Sometimes burdens arrive as an unexpected turn of event. A tragedy, trauma, or life-altering situation that raises awareness of something that was barely on the radar beforehand. The sudden turn of events and new reality become a cause that needs correction. An injustice to make right. A societal burden that needs to be alleviated. Because of what we have experienced and because it has touched something deep within us, it now becomes our life's work to make sure something is done about the problem, whatever it may be. In essence, it becomes our purpose and mission in life.

Prayer is often the repository for our burdens. Whatever is weighing heavily on our hearts becomes the script for our prayers. In this chapter we look at a burden that triggered a simple prayer, which ultimately led to a dramatic turn of events. Not only for the person who bore the burden in the first place, but for an entire nation.

Burdened by the News

The story of Nehemiah in the Old Testament is a fascinating one. Very little if anything is known of his years prior to his introduction to the book that bears his name. Though the successes and leadership lessons of Nehemiah are well documented elsewhere, one detail rarely receives the notice it deserves, despite the fact that without it, the life of Nehemiah would have unfolded very differently.

The time in which Nehemiah lived saw the Jewish exiles begin their return to Jerusalem to repair and restore the city that had been originally decimated by the Babylonians when they carted the majority of the nation into exile in 586–587 BC. The Temple had been rebuilt, albeit a shadow of its former glory. But the walls, the important fortifications for the safety of the city continued to lie in ruins.

The opening verses of Nehemiah have him questioning those returning from Judah about the condition of Jerusalem and of those who survived the exile. The news that the city's walls and gates lay in ruin, drives Nehemiah to weep. In his grief, he commits to fasting and prayer and it is here that we need to take a closer look.

It is approximately 140 years since the destruction of Jerusalem by the Babylonian king, Nebuchadnezzar. That is the span of time that exists when Nehemiah enters the scene. In fact, based on anything we can ascertain, Nehemiah has never seen Jerusalem to witness the devastation firsthand. Yet, despite no first-hand knowledge, he is gutted by what he hears.

By all accounts, Nehemiah has likely always lived in the land of those who exiled his ancestors. His roots to his heritage and his people run deep. He knows well the implications of a ruined city that was once the capital of a nation birthed by the sovereign hand of God. The news of its fate stirs something deep within Nehemiah and births in him a compulsion that is going to dramatically alter the course of his life.

Moved to Action

Earlier in this chapter we introduced the idea of a burden and how it can reframe the priorities of our life. For Nehemiah, the condition of Jerusalem was a burden he could not ignore or pretend did not exist. He felt compelled to take action. To do something, anything. Physically, Nehemiah is removed by hundreds of miles from the city. From his present home in Susa, Jerusalem was about an eight-day journey away. It is one thing to have a burden, it's another thing altogether to be relatively helpless in doing anything about it.

Nehemiah, so weighed down, could have simply let the matter remain a sad reality. It would have been easy to justify in his own mind: "What can I do?" Though, as cup-bearer to the king, Nehemiah would have had a lot of power, likely equal to the ranks of a general at the very least. Yet, in the hands of a weaker person, the nature of the task would have seemed too daunting to see it through to the end. All good ideas die for lack of either motivation, resources, or execution, and Nehemiah wasn't going to let anything stand in the way.

Undeterred, Nehemiah, rather than focus on what he was unable to do, took the only course of action available to him. He

Heavy Waits

committed the entire matter to prayer. This was not just a good idea to Nehemiah, it was a God-given and God-shaped burden. It became an imperative, a get-it-done-at-any-cost imperative. Jerusalem could no longer lie as a city that was a shadow of its former self. With such an imperative weighing on his heart, Nehemiah began to pray. He prayed for four months and the script is given below. It is a lesson in prayer, not only for what it says, but for what it doesn't say.

> [5] Then I said, "O LORD, God of heaven, the great and awesome God who keeps his covenant of unfailing love with those who love him and obey his commands, [6] listen to my prayer! Look down and see me praying night and day for your people Israel. I confess that we have sinned against you. Yes, even my own family and I have sinned! [7] We have sinned terribly by not obeying the commands, decrees, and regulations that you gave us through your servant Moses. [8] "Please remember what you told your servant Moses: 'If you are unfaithful to me, I will scatter you among the nations. [9] But if you return to me and obey my commands and live by them, then even if you are exiled to the ends of the earth, I will bring you back to the place I have chosen for my name to be honored.' [10] "The people you rescued by your great power and strong hand are your servants. [11] O Lord, please hear my prayer! Listen to the prayers of those of us who delight in honoring you. Please grant me success today by making the king favorable to me. Put it into his heart to be kind to me." In those days I was the king's cup-bearer. (Nehemiah 1:1–11)

Nehemiah's prayer is surprising on many fronts. His acknowledgement of the nation's sin, as well as his own, frames the entire prayer as an open admission of Israel's present condition. They had not been faithful to the stipulations of the covenant, and exile became the result of their disobedience. The fact that the Jewish people had been exiled would be cause for great shame. The prayer demonstrates Nehemiah's understanding of the covenant God formed with the nation—not only the negative aspects due to disobedience, but also the positive blessings that obedience would offer.

Asking with Intent

It's to the positive aspects that Nehemiah appeals. As much as God has proven his sovereignty to bring about the nation's exile, the same is true about the Lord's promise of bringing those who are obedient back. Nehemiah, recognizing his own inabilities to bring about the desired outcome of his burden for Jerusalem, appeals to the one who can. It is because of the present reality of the nation that Nehemiah can pray so openly for the reversal of the nation's fortunes. As much as the exile was foretold, the return was equally foretold.

This confidence that Nehemiah exhibits in his prayer is tempered by humility. Nehemiah could have asked for the walls to have been rebuilt in a number of different ways. "Lord, raise up an army to get the job done." "Move the heart of the people to fund the project." Nehemiah could have appealed for God to work in a myriad of miraculous ways but there is nothing in the prayer that evokes any direct appeal for the city or its walls. Instead, the prayer ends on an appeal that is somewhat unexpected.

He simply asks to have the king respond favorably when Nehemiah approaches him. In an interesting twist, it is at the conclusion of the prayer that we even find out Nehemiah's position as the king's cupbearer, an important position that put him within the ranks of those the king would see as loyal and trustworthy. Due to Nehemiah's responsibility and importance, his position within the court is hard not to see as providential.

Yet, for all of Nehemiah's intimate contact with the king, he assumes nothing in the way of privileges or rights. Nehemiah prays that God would give him "success" before the king, using a Hebrew word denoting "to prosper." Nehemiah prayed for four months, and all he wanted was an opportunity to share his burden with the one person who stood between Nehemiah and a restored

Jerusalem. Nehemiah knew it would take divine intervention for such an opportunity to present itself.

Our tendency is to pray for miracles, but in reality, we likely need to be praying more for opportunities. Those open-door moments that are made available to us where God is seen as working intimately with the details of our life. In our impatience, we want to see the entire bloom before a seed is ever planted. Granted, there are moments when our prayers are desperate for miraculous intervention, but how often do we ignore the simpler and more mundane steps needed to bring something to its end result? What if there is something in the process that God is trying to teach us?

In the case of Nehemiah, he needed the king on his side. With him as an obstacle, whatever burden Nehemiah carried would become either a dead weight that grew heavier over time, or a regret when years of inaction were recalled to memory.

Weighing the Risks

When Nehemiah heard of the conditions of the city, he wept openly. God was beginning to paint a picture in the heart of Nehemiah of what God wanted to accomplish. When a burden is God-shaped and God-ordained, to not see it through will feel like utter failure and spiritual collapse. A God given burden becomes mission critical.

Reading the story of Nehemiah, we can miss the danger that he faced in approaching the king, a conversation that could have been his last. It's this realization that would have prompted Nehemiah's prayer request in the first place. The singular focus of his prayer was for success, nothing more and nothing less. Nehemiah knew the potential risks all too well, which is likely the reason for his four months of petitioning the Lord. Oftentimes when we bypass the risks, we can forfeit the miraculous working of God in our lives.

Nehemiah modelled in those four months an ability to trust and patiently wait upon the Lord. I think it would be easy to imagine Nehemiah playing over and over in his head the conversations he would have with the king. It's very possible he played out a variety of scenarios with an equal variety of potential outcomes. It is in the waiting where the enormity of a burden can bring to mind feelings of trepidation and anxiety. God-shaped burdens have a way of making us swallow hard. But the season of waiting, however long or short, is also the time where God is building in us the spiritual and moral compulsion for what he wants to accomplish through us.

The period of prayerfully waiting also produces a sense of alignment. Good ideas, over time, will become even more compelling. God-shaped burdens, over time, become mission critical. The time allows Nehemiah's heart to become fully aligned with God's, and the mission a crucial part of Nehemiah's obedience. There's no turning back for Nehemiah, no matter the consequences he could likely face. Whenever we are given the potential for significant change or for changing the world for the better, the reality of risk is not far behind.

With all things that are mission critical, the time will eventually come to put desire into action. For Nehemiah, the months of prayer have not abated the desire to see the matter through. The conviction appears to have grown even more and so to the king he must go. When he does finally approach the king, it is prompted by the king asking Nehemiah why he looks like a man with deep troubles. The moment of truth, the moment that has consumed four months of prayer, has arrived.

Success and More

To say that God answered Nehemiah's prayer is an understatement. The fact the king did not have him removed from service at best or executed at worst, testifies to this. He agreed to not only let Nehemiah go to the city but gave letters of endorsement as well. Add to that the king sending military officials to escort Nehemiah and the simple prayer request of Nehemiah for success has been met and surpassed. In due time, the broken walls that weighed down the heart of Nehemiah are rebuilt, and the city once again restored.

Imagine what this would have done for the people of Israel, whether those in exiled lands or those who had been left behind in the ruins. It would have heralded a new day where God was once again looking favorably upon them. The scourge of the exile was now an historical footnote, and the fortunes of the nation looked hopeful, more so than they had for some time. All because of one man, one burden, one prayer.

Though Nehemiah was removed by hundreds of miles from his native Jerusalem, he was so burdened by its condition that he began to pray. That prayer became the catalyst for a restoration and building program that changed the fate of the entire Jewish people. In many ways, it could be argued that Nehemiah's position as cupbearer to the king was a natural opportunity to influence him, without the need for prayer at all. After-all, could you not argue God placed him there for that very reason?

As presumptuous as that may be, leaving God out of the equation was not an option for Nehemiah. The need was too great, the risks too large, and the necessity of success too critical to leave it to human ingenuity or any other factors such as luck or chance. This was not a time for human arrogance to get in the way. There was going to be one shot at this, and it had better count. If Nehemiah was to see any progress forward, he had to pray.

Nehemiah's prayer is a model of humility and of recognizing the importance of acknowledging God's glory and reputation. Yes, the city walls were going to be a haven once again for the people and install practical protection for those within its gates. But for Nehemiah, the city and its temple were representative of the glory of God. To have them lie in ruins was an affront that could no longer be tolerated. To elevate the Lord to his rightful place brought not only success to Nehemiah but hope for all the people of God everywhere.

What do we do when a burden weighs heavy on our hearts? Our first thoughts may very well be, "What can I do about it"? We can feel it's beyond our ability to effect any significant changes.

Even small challenges can seem daunting or overwhelming at times. But to leave God out of the equation should never be an option, especially in moments when everything appears stacked against us.

From a human standpoint, if we neglect the potential for God to do the impossible it can create in us a posture of helplessness. Helplessness left lingering too long soon turns into hopelessness and despair. And when a burden is large and daunting, the more it will challenge our human capacity to do nothing about it. Why not risk God potentially doing the impossible, or at least something beyond our wildest expectations?

There are times when prayer is the only thing we can do about the matters that burden our hearts. But rather than seeing prayer as a last resort, maybe it's better to see it as the best resort, especially in matters that seem so far beyond our natural abilities to correct. What would happen if we became burdened in our prayer lives for the glory of God to be made evident not only in our churches, but in every nation of the world?

4

Enemy at the Gate

Fear has become the great enemy of our age. Countless resources, from podcasts to personal wellness gurus, warn of the potential dangers when fear is allowed to run wild. It's the one emotion, we are warned, that we do not want controlling our life. When it does, we quickly find ourselves trapped in a prison of our own making. Fear becomes the darkroom of our mind, manufacturing countless scenarios of negative outcomes that leave us incapacitated and paralyzed. To triumph over fear, is to prevail over every impediment life will throw our way.

Few groups have warned of the potential dangers of fear more than those claiming biblical faith. After all, isn't the admonition to not fear, a common refrain throughout the Scriptures? Have we not been told that the Bible contains the phrase, "Do not fear", some 365 times, one for each day of the year? With so much censure, can anything good come out of fear?

Few emotions have been demonized or weaponized, as much as fear. How many of us have been chastised by a well-meaning believer to have faith over fear? A simple yet loaded statement that somehow is supposed to quell the horror we feel as we face a life-threatening situation. Few emotions have garnered as much negative press as fear, while at the same time being commonly experienced by everyone, regardless of religious persuasion.

Granted, fear definitely has many negative characteristics, and many valid reasons to limit its effects, but to treat it as wholly negative without any redeeming quality is to miss its more subtle purposes. What are we to do with biblical figures like Elijah, who was wracked with fear when threatened by Jezebel (1 Kings 19:3), or Moses at the burning bush (Exodus 3:6)? What of the apostle Paul, who admits to being fearful when first entering the city of Corinth (1 Cor. 2:3)? Even David, the one who slew Goliath, was gripped by moments of fear (1 Sam. 21:12; 2 Sam. 6:9).How could these incredible examples of faith allow such an emotion so harmful to their spiritual health take hold of them?

What do we make of the common refrain within the wisdom literature of the Bible, that to fear the Lord is the beginning of wisdom (Psalm 111:10; Proverbs 1:7; 2:5; 9:10 to cite a few passages)? How can fear even dare to coexist with wisdom, let alone point us to God? One way it is reconciled is by limiting the definition of fear in these contexts as meaning, reverence, respect, or an idiom for worship. Even if we were to limit the semantic range of fear, the implication of the wisdom literature is that there is a sacredness to fear. Limiting the term fear to worship alone, neutralizes the intent of the text, because there is always an element of being afraid of God.

Putting Fear in its Place

We rarely think of fear in a positive light, yet we use it on a daily basis to guide us and guard us from potential risk and harm. We do not think twice about putting an infant in a car seat and ensuring that they are safely strapped in. Somehow, legitimate fears that prompt us to take wise action escape our definition when applied to a spiritual context? Remember, earlier we stated the popular idea that the Bible contains a "Do not fear" for every day of the year. I don't know who or how that started, but it's simply not true. In my own study, I got at best 29, but have seen others get as high as 50. It all depends on the translation and criteria you use, but to state it as 365 times is an easily provable exaggeration.

Fear does have a place, in fact, a very important place. It triggers our warning system and when it does, there is often a choice to be made. We either allow the fear to wash over us and succumb to it, or we use it to move us into action. It's at this juncture that the admonitions in Scripture against fear begin to take shape. When we are encouraged to "fear not" in Scripture, it is not leaving us on our own, or without valid options.

In fact, to treat faith and fear as opposites, and even as enemies, is troubling. There are two ways that fear complements faith. Firstly, when a situation arises that provokes fear, Scripture encourages us to not allow the haunting questions and dark possibilities that fear invites but to use that fear to turn to God. Fear has the ability to make us a hostage of our own imaginations. Fear, for all its cultural warnings, serves as a signpost that is pointing us to God.

Secondly, fear is a type of value assessment tool. It can reveal what you value most, or at the very least what holds priority in your life. For instance, if you fear losing your job, or fear for the safety of your children, it points to those areas of your life that have value. It is not that these fears are inherently wrong, but they are meant to prompt us to wise actions. In these cases, if we allowed fear to govern our response to our work, or our children, we would soon be overcome with worry, anxiety, and stress.

Fear, surrendered to God, becomes a tool that he can use to build our faith and dependency on him, and over time, the fears that typically paralyze others will instead become a catalyst for prayer and sage action for those of us who are relying on him.

When a Threat Appears

In Isaiah chapters 36–37, the Assyrian army has landed on the doorstep of Jerusalem. They have steamrolled across adjoining lands, capturing every nation in their path, and now they have set their sights on the city of Jerusalem. Few have been able to withstand the onslaught of the Assyrian nation at the time. For king

Hezekiah, the prospect of the Assyrians surrounding the city is one no king ever wants to face.

The mouthpiece for Sennacherib, the Assyrian king, is a man designated in Hebrew as Rabshakeh, a term for someone who is a chief of staff, a commander, or even a cupbearer for the king. King Hezekiah's officials watch as he approaches and, in a clear demonstration of intimidation and psychological warfare, lays out the dire situation that the city and her king now face. The shrewdness of the commander is shown in his decision to speak in common Hebrew, not in the Aramaic language of the diplomats, so that all upon the walls of the city could hear the insults and the threats.

The commander pronounces a warning that the God of Israel will not protect them and assure the people that they do not have the military manpower to win. Nor will Egypt come to their aid. He even makes a claim too impossible to be believed: Assyria has authority from Yahweh, the God of Israel, to attack Jerusalem. He mocks any strategy devised by Hezekiah as lacking not only in wisdom, but the means to fulfill it. In a final stroke of humiliation, the commander even offers Hezekiah two-thousand horses, as a way of illustrating the inferiority of the Israelite army.

Since every nation and every god they claimed has already fallen to the might of the Assyrians, Jerusalem and Judah will too. If Hezekiah knew what was best, he would surrender the city. As king, the fate of the city now rests on what the king does next. No one, absolutely no one, would have blamed Hezekiah for the fear that he must have felt as the city was surrounded by the encampments of Assyrian soldiers.

The lives of an entire city—men, woman, and children—are at stake. The reputation of the fabled city of Jerusalem, the city of God, also lies in the balance. The king, having retreated to the temple, has inquired of the well-known prophet Isaiah who has assured him that the Lord will protect Israel.

This is the juncture where fear and faith meet. On one hand, the city has a mortal enemy at its gates, while on the other, a prophet's proclamation of "fear not." Besides Isaiah's words of assurance, he also reveals that the Lord has already determined the fate of the Assyrian king—that death awaits him when he returns to his own country.

Faith Propelled by Fear

At this point in the story, one would assume that the script has already been written. Isaiah has pronounced Yahweh's judgement so all that needs to happen is to wait and watch the Lord fulfill his word. As stereotypical as that may sound, another scene is added to the story with its central focus, not on the ongoing machinations of the Assyrians as they continue their taunts and threats, but on the prayer of Hezekiah.

While the Assyrians' attention is diverted to other military matters, they still have the wherewithal to deliver a letter spelling out in writing the threats that have been verbalized so far. With the arrival of the letter, Hezekiah once again heads for the temple—the place designated as the house of prayer. The scene in Isaiah chapter 37 as Hezekiah enters the temple not only conveys the heart of a godly king, but also the beauty of prayer when fear propels faith.

Hezekiah, having heard from the prophet, could have set aside any need for prayer. Though it may not have come across as such, it would have evoked a type of arrogance or a type of expectation from God that would have bordered on presumption. After all, the Assyrians had yet to disappear and, by all accounts, were not going to be leaving anytime soon. Beginning in verse 14 of chapter 37, we have the prayer of Hezekiah:

> [14] After Hezekiah received the letter from the messengers and read it, he went up to the LORD's Temple and spread it out before the LORD. [15] And Hezekiah prayed this prayer before the LORD: [16] "O LORD of Heaven's Armies, God of Israel, you are enthroned between the mighty cherubim! You alone are God of all the kingdoms of the earth. You alone created the heavens and the earth. [17] Bend down, O LORD, and listen! Open your eyes, O LORD, and see! Listen to Sennacherib's words of defiance against the living God. (Isaiah 37:14–17)

The letter has all the markings of a credible threat and as Hezekiah comes into the temple he spreads out the letter before the Lord. This simple act by the king is an expression of shock and outrage, a way of saying, "Are you going to let this go unanswered"? What follows is a simple prayer with profound implications.

His prayer revolves around three basic categories, all three of which are hotly contested in our post-Christian world. The first is that of God as creator. In our present environment, the rift between science and creationism has a long and tattered history and one that will continue well into the future. Regardless, to acknowledge this as a believer is to acknowledge the responsibility we have as caretakers of the world we live in.

The second is God as king. To most, the language of king and kingdom is a throwback to a bygone era. But the imagery cannot be ignored in the context of Hezekiah, a king who is acknowledging the greater king, the one who rules all of creation. Likewise, as believers, we may not use the terminology of kingship, but all the imagery of the position exists as we release our lives to the authority and power of our heavenly father. As we are beholden to God as creator, we are also accountable to God as our king.

The third is God as personal. This last characteristic makes all the difference. God is creator and king, but it doesn't mean he has to care about his creation, or the people who are part of it. But God does care about the details of our lives and longs to be in relationship with us. For Hezekiah, God is concerned not only for the welfare of the people who claim his name, but for the way the Assyrians are defying the living God. Hezekiah's prayer is not so much about getting out of a jam, but about what this will do to God's reputation. It is here we turn to the closing section of his prayer.

> [18] "It is true, LORD, that the kings of Assyria have destroyed all these nations. [19] And they have thrown the gods of these nations into the fire and burned them. But of course the Assyrians could destroy them! They were not gods at all--only idols of wood and stone shaped by human hands. [20] Now, O LORD our God, rescue us from

his power; then all the kingdoms of the earth will know that you alone, O LORD, are God." (Isa 37:18-20)

The last section of Hezekiahs' prayer is where the big ask takes place. It's a prayer for God to rescue the people but with an important addition. Rescue us so that, "all the kingdoms of the earth will know that you alone, O Lord, are God." Given the enormity of the situation faced by Hezekiah and the fear it must have evoked, not only in the king but in his people too, the fact that he was equally concerned about God being glorified and vindicated is important to note.

The Value of Fear

How many of us qualify our prayers in this way? What if our prayers are pleading for God to protect newborns from abortions on demand? Do we equally pray, not only for the saving of a precious child, but also that it would demonstrate to the world that to God, every single child matters? That we are all made in his image, and all are wonderfully knitted by the master's hand, deserving of a life that God has purposed? No child is an accident to God.

Maybe our prayers are centered around social justice. Are we praying for communities that have been torn by racial strife to find peace and learn to live together or are we also praying that through the reconciliation process people will see the gracious hand of God on every person, regardless of race or ethnicity? God is a God of justice for all.

Maybe we are struggling in our marriage. What difference would it make if we didn't just pray for the Lord to change me or my spouse but instead focused the prayer differently? What if our prayer went more like this: "Lord, guard this relationship for your names sake. You instituted marriage and made it a picture of what society can be like when love and faithfulness are confined between two who become one. Guard it, Lord, because if we are to fail, we will become another statistic for those who say marriage is dated and should be open to reinterpretation. What shame would that bring to that which you created from the beginning"?

Most, if not all, of our social issues, revolve in some way around the fear factor—fear of rejection, fear of commitment, fear of those not like us, and even fear of success. No wonder fear is so readily maligned whenever it rears its ugly head. There are countless fears, phobias, and related anxieties that are causing a health care crisis in many societies. What we are saying is that we need to pay attention to our fears, and use them as a catalyst for trusting God.

Hezekiah had a choice—allow his fear to determine how he was going to manage the looming threat on his doorstep, or seek the Lord. In some ways, fear helps frame reality for Hezekiah. In his prayer he acknowledges the power and might of the Assyrians, recognizing that their threat is not hollow, but their theology is. For all the might of the Assyrians, it was wrong of them to think for a moment that they were defeating real gods, when in fact, they were worthless idols.

Fear has a tendency to become irrational and overrun us when faith is absent. Besides, without faith what options do we have? Muscle through it, ignore it, or succumb to it. In every case the fear has controlled us in some way. Hezekiah's option is to recognize the validity of the fear, yet transfer the management of it to the Lord.

God will meet us where our fear has already taken us. He is not disconnected to what is happening around us or inside us. As mentioned earlier, fear has a way of acting as a signpost, warning us of real threats and real areas of concern. However, they need not consume us.

Hezekiah's prayer became the catalyst for the saving of the people of Israel from a real and credible threat. If we read the rest of the story, God destroyed and scattered the Assyrians and even made good on his revelation of the Assyrian king's fate. God is the God who will act on our fears, if we are open to releasing them to him.

It is reasonable to assert that Hezekiah's fear would not have been totally alleviated until he witnessed the defeat and retreat of the Assyrian army. Does this mean that Hezekiah was not trusting God, or does it teach us that often, in the midst of what we fear, we can also be trusting God for the outcome? Though faith and fear are often treated as enemies, fear, understood properly, can help us not only lean into God, but also deepen our faith and trust in Him.

Equal to Hezekiah's fear of the Assyrian army at his doorstep was his fear of an outcome that would defame the name of the Lord. Prayer is never meant to be a refuge of last resort, but an ongoing expression of our faith in God to do the impossible for his sake, as well as ours. Prayer should elevate God, but in a culture of self above all else, we can sometimes forget to put the Lord in his proper place.

5

OTHER-WORLDLY

I REMEMBER AS A young boy the day my mother told me she had a gift for me. Imagine my surprise when she handed me a large ornate silver cross. My original thought when she intimated a gift was something more in line with a young boy, like a new bike.

The cross that she presented to me was no ordinary cross, but one that had been blessed by the orthodox priest at the church. My mom took the cross and placed it between the mattresses of my bed. This, she assured me, was to protect my soul, and ward off any evil spirits and demons that would terrorize me in the night.

To my young mind, the thought that my room was now a haven for demonic spirits guaranteed more than a few restless nights. How would I ever get another peaceful night's rest knowing that my room was a potential haven for dark spirits?

The crowning jewel of her generosity to me that day was a second gift, a picture of Jesus. She hung it directly opposite my bed so every night it was the last face I would see before falling asleep. My mom was now confident that my soul was safe, at least from whatever dark influences lurked in my room.

To this day, I am convinced that the eyes of Jesus in that picture would follow me as I walked around my room. It was an eerie sensation to experience. Countless nights I would lie in bed and ponder the spiritual world and the questions I had about its existence and what actually transpired in the world between heaven and earth. Little did my mom realize what she awoke in me that day?

The Great Beyond

That was my first experience with any concept of a spiritual world, at least in a way that made me aware of something more than the limitations of our physical world. Years later, when I began to interact with the Bible, I was once again reminded that the spiritual realm was no abstraction for its writers, but an ever-present reality that affected our lives more than we imagined.

The particular passage that serves as our focus opens the curtain to the spiritual realm, particularly in terms of what transpires in that realm when we pray. The question we're asking is, "What do we invite when we pray?" Whether believer or non-believer, we tend to believe that when we pray it is this intimate conversation between God and ourselves.

The Bible seems to hold a slightly different view. Yes, it's true that our prayers are communion with God, but something else potentially happens in the spiritual world. As we look at a passage in Daniel, the implications are that other spiritual forces are incited whenever we pray. Daniel 10 is one of those rare passages in the Bible that pulls the curtain away from the physical world and allows us a glimpse into the mysterious realm of the spiritual world.

First, let me give you a little background to set the stage. Daniel 9 and 10 are written in the genre of apocalyptic literature. Anyone familiar with interpreting this type of literature knows it is fraught with potential problems. How literal do we take the imagery, typology, and allusions that predominate the genre and the messages it attempts to convey? The attempt here is to be sensitive to the pitfalls of interpreting apocalyptic prose while at the same time extracting the valuable truths that lay within, especially as it relates to the subject of prayer.

In the beginning of chapter 10, Daniel is with a group at the banks of the Tigress River. Amid his fasting and praying, he perceives a man standing there. No one else in the group sees the man except for Daniel. He describes the person starting at verse 4:

> [4] On April 23, as I was standing on the bank of the great Tigris River, [5] I looked up and saw a man dressed in linen clothing, with a belt of pure gold around his waist. [6] His body looked like a precious gem. His face flashed like lightning, and his eyes flamed like torches. His arms and feet shone like polished bronze, and his voice roared like a vast multitude of people. (Daniel 10:4–6)

Those with Daniel do not see the vision but are terrified by the sound and flee. Daniel is left alone and collapses from the encounter. The man revives Daniel and relates that he has a message from God. He begins by stating that Daniel is very precious to God. This detail is not insignificant to the narrative. It places Daniel in a context of status. Due to Daniel's deep reverence, he has endeared himself to the Lord, and therefore is being used in God's progressive plan.

The messenger has a revelation for Daniel on the future state of the nation of Israel. A vision that the messenger has come to communicate so Daniel, as God's prophet, can pass it on to the nation itself. Though the future that is presented is important, the focus of this particular chapter is on the details that the messenger gives concerning what transpired when attempting to deliver it. The key verses are found in Daniel 10:12–14.

> [12] Then he said, "Don't be afraid, Daniel. Since the first day you began to pray for understanding and to humble yourself before your God, your request has been heard in heaven. I have come in answer to your prayer. [13] But for twenty-one days the spirit prince of the kingdom of Persia blocked my way. Then Michael, one of the archangels, came to help me, and I left him there with the spirit prince of the kingdom of Persia. [14] Now I am here to explain what will happen to your people in the future, for this vision concerns a time yet to come." (Daniel 10:12–14)

Few biblical passages confront the dynamics of the spiritual world as directly as these. And though Daniel would receive an explanation as to the delay in hearing his prayers answered, most of us are never fully cognizant of what's invoked whenever we petition God through our prayers.

It begs the question then, "What do we invite when we pray"? In the midst of Daniel's prayers, as he fasts and mourns for twenty-one days, events are unleashed that he cannot possibly imagine. In the quietness of his time with God, the unseen world is propelled into a cosmic battle that is initiated by the very requests that Daniel presents to the Lord. Events so dramatic, they would consume every media outlet if they were played out in the physical world.

More Than Just Touched by An Angel

Daniel has been praying, fasting, and mourning for three weeks. For twenty-one consecutive days, he has come before God, undoubtedly bearing a great burden. In the previous chapter (9), Daniel was given a vision of the future, a revelation that would have predominated the thoughts and petitions of Daniel.

Upon the angel reviving Daniel and setting him back on his feet, the admonition is given to not be afraid, a natural response given the weight and otherworldliness of such events. There are a couple of notable features that follow in the commentary given by the angel. The first is the angel's confirmation that the moment Daniel began to pray the request was heard in heaven and the angel was dispatched in response. It's interesting that there is no time lag for God. He answered the prayer and sent the messenger right away. It was immediate.

The response to the prayer did not go to committee or get vetted through a process. God's answer to Daniel was quick and deliberate. The message that the angel is delivering to Daniel concerns important details in the future. All orchestrated by God. All determined by him.

Notice that Daniel, in his prayer, is asking God for one thing alone. His petition to God is this: he desires understanding. I believe this to be significant. Many times, we are praying to God and asking him specifically for answers concerning real and tangible needs. Yet in this case Daniel, cognizant of the needs, asks not for answers but for understanding.

The section here in Daniel is the third of three visions. He must have been overwhelmed by the sheer enormity of God's revelation and what the future held for the nation of Israel and the world. Remember, the context in Daniel is the oppressed people of God who are living in exile. Only recently has the nation begun to experience the waning of God's judgment upon them, but Daniel has been privileged to see the future as much more.

Many times, we don't understand the circumstances around us. We don't understand the context of what is happening or why. But prayer is a wonderful way of asking God to help put our circumstances in context for us. Another way to say this is that life needs to be interpreted. If we did not have the word of God, we would interpret our lives purely by the circumstances around us. Sometimes it is very hard to see clearly within the haze that oftentimes envelopes our lives.

For Daniel, his prayer is for discernment, clarity, and wisdom. The revelation of God demands no less. The Hebrew is instructive in its force. What is translated, as "understanding" is more than just mental ascent. It is the heart of Daniel being impacted by the visions, which causes him to respond in reverent fear and obedience. He not only serves as a privileged prophet of key information, but one who is deeply moved by it to the core of his being.

It can become easy to view life through the influences and circumstances around us. The people who are closest, the culture we live in, or our own flawed perceptions. The word of God helps us to interpret life as God intends us to see it, but life is often interpreted by what is easily perceived around us—what we are able to touch, taste, smell, or feel.

Prayer helps us to see life interpreted through God eyes, through God's will. Many times, we just need to understand what is happening to us in light of God's promises, in light of God's hope, and not allow those circumstances to be the determining factor of our relationship with God. What we may be experiencing now is part of God's program. It may be hurtful. It may be hard to take. It may be causing us to question. But the prayers end up becoming an opportunity for us to interrupt our lives based on God's word. And this is where Daniel is praying, to understand how these visions should be interpreted in light of God's plan for mankind and Israel.

Locked and Loaded

Beginning in verse 13 we come to the next point. Prayer can also incite evil to counteract the actions and purposes of God. Our prayers become a provocation for the devil and his minions, an aspect of prayer that is rarely considered.

When Daniel begins fasting and praying, a heavenly messenger is sent out right away. But the messenger is delayed for twenty-one days because of an evil spirit, an evil prince who is actually a territorial prince governing the region of Persia. There is a battle, a war that is happening. Even the archangel Michael has come to help.

If you read further, in verse 20, the angel acknowledges that upon his return, he will once again not only face the prince of Persia but the prince of Greece as well. So, the battle continues. Here we have a clear example in the Bible that when we pray, things happen. The battle for good and evil continues. It's a tremendous war zone, this arena we know as the spiritual realm.

And it is sometimes a difficult thing for us to fathom. Here is Daniel, one of the most godly saints in the Bible who is highly favored by the Lord, who lives in perfect obedience, yet his prayers invoke this great battle in the heavenlies. A battle he would be unaware of had God not pulled back the curtain for just a few brief moments.

An interesting lesson here when it comes to prayer is that delays are not necessarily denials. Just because we do not see the answer to prayer right away does not mean that God has delayed in answering it. The delay could be a result of the battle that ensues in the spiritual realm that we are totally unaware of. Here is one way to think of this—whenever we pray, we invite the potential for battle. We saw in an earlier chapter with king Jehoshaphat that when it comes to battle, it belongs to the Lord.

In our modern, scientifically driven world we want measurable, quantifiable statistics. The spirit realm for many of us is a reality we don't know what to do with, let alone how to manage. We may not understand it all, but the implication from passages such as the one in Daniel points to an ongoing war. Prayer is the communication device across enemy lines, and it is important that we at least acknowledge it.

The battle we see around us physically is just a snapshot of the greater war that is being waged in the spiritual realm. Sometimes, what seems very small and insignificant has greater weight in the spiritual world. Our prayers should embrace the larger arena and the larger perspective than just our immediate circumstances reveal.

One valid reason for encouraging this awareness is the potential to view elements of our life as not needing prayer. We may think of a particular issue as a small thing yet in reality, in the spiritual realm, it may constitute a much larger conflict.

In our science saturated world, we tend to see life at a manageable level. But often there is more behind what is in front of us. I think it is one of the reasons some do not want to pray or do not find it important enough because it just doesn't motivate them. They don't understand what is really going on or the fierceness of the battle that is being waged in the background.

Tactical Advantage

One of the more memorable passages dealing with this topic is found in Ephesians 6:11–12, a New Testament passage that speaks to the nature of the battle:

> [11] Put on all of God's armor so that you will be able to stand firm against all strategies of the devil. [12] For we are not fighting against flesh-and-blood enemies, but against

evil rulers and authorities of the unseen world, against mighty powers in this dark world, and against evil spirits in the heavenly places. (Ephesians 6:11–12)

The apostle Paul graphically depicts the warfare as requiring God's spiritual armor, because the nature of the battle is spiritual. It is not just flesh and blood warfare. What we physically experience all around us is just the tip of the iceberg. The armor that God provides is part of the preparation for battle, as is prayer, in order that we can stand against whatever the devil throws at us.

What is so daunting is that the greater battle being waged is in the arena we know the least about. Any tactician will tell you the importance of good intel for military engagement. Yet when it comes to spiritual warfare, prayer is the primary weapon that we wield. One that essentially entrusts God with the battle plan and its outcome.

If you are a believer, you have to understand that you are going to be attacked. Make no mistake, it will happen with certainty. But just as certain is the assurance that God is in the fight on our behalf. As much as prayer can invite the potential for a battle, we are not left to fight alone. Nor are we destined for defeat, as the apostle Paul reminds us in Colossians when he writes,

> [13] You were dead because of your sins and because your sinful nature was not yet cut away. Then God made you alive with Christ, for he forgave all our sins. [14] He canceled the record of the charges against us and took it away by nailing it to the cross. [15] In this way, he disarmed the spiritual rulers and authorities. He shamed them publicly by his victory over them on the cross. (Col. 2:13–15)

It is one thing to recognize the victory; it is another thing entirely to live it. As believers, we can easily acknowledge mentally the theological truths that anchor our faith, yet to live them within the turmoil of a fallen and dark world can be a challenge. How often do we live victorious lives, free of the lies of the devil?

Satan's name translates as accuser or adversary, descriptions befitting his character. Jesus calls him the father of lies and a liar from the beginning (John 8:44). In terms of what can be guaranteed to come whenever the devil attacks you, it will undoubtedly be rooted in deception, falsehood, and outright lies.

In one sense, part of spiritual growth is nothing more than replacing lies with truth. At the very least, spiritual warfare is a battle between truth and falsehoods. It is the most basic attack we can expect and one that is aimed squarely at faith. We see this in the words of the apostle Paul when he writes in Ephesians, "In addition to all of these, hold up the shield of faith to stop the fiery arrows of the devil" (Ephesians 6:16).

Though a battle is being waged in the spiritual realm, the effects of the fighting are felt in the physical realm. I believe that God's primary concern for humanity is our faith. So, it is not surprising that the Ephesians 6 passage stresses that same faith as a means of protection. Conversely, it is not surprising that it would also be a crucial target for the devil.

Therein lies the heart of the war that ensues in the spiritual realm. As seen in the passage from Daniel, the unseen world is one where the forces of good and evil are in constant conflict. How is it that the forces of darkness were even aware of Daniel's prayer? Was it seeing the release of the heavenly angels that gave notice to the enemy in the first place?

For Daniel, he personally experiences a delayed response to his prayers, and fortunately for him, he receives an answer as to why. How many of us have wondered about delayed responses to our own prayers, even though we acknowledge as a theological principle that God's timing is always perfect? (See 2 Sam. 22:31; Psalm 18:30).

None of this is to negate the sovereignty of God or his power over the dark forces of this world, but it does acknowledge the reality of the conflict that exists. Is it fair to extrapolate from the text of Daniel a general principle concerning the spiritual world and apply it to our own prayer life? One has to wonder what purpose the Daniel text serves, beyond its historical context and importance, if not as a hint to the power of the unseen world, one that we are mostly unaware of.

Not for the Faint of Heart

We may not fully understand what exists behind the veil of the spiritual realm, but based on the text of Daniel, an epic battle between good and evil rages on. Our prayers, in some way, play a role. What we can ascertain is that the devil will undermine any and every attempt we make to live righteous, faithful, and godly lives.

So, what are we to make of such awareness? For one, it should prompt us to acknowledge that we should never be comfortable in our prayers. We are soldiers of a battle that is ensuing in the heavenlies. We need to recognize that prayer is not a docile practice but an inflammatory gesture at the devil, with the potential to incite a war.

When it comes to the matter of spiritual warfare, there are generally two extremes that exist. The first is stressing everything is of the devil while the other is totally discounting his involvement altogether. The balance exists in being cognizant of the reality lying somewhere in the middle. My tendency is to say that we lean more towards the extreme of ignoring the devil. This may be the more harmful of the two extremes, primarily because it allows the devil to play fast and loose without our ability to recognize or even acknowledge an attack when it comes.

Because we can be uncomfortable with the subject of spiritual warfare, we don't want to give it the kind of attention it deserves. Yet, doing so may be a way of encouraging the people of God to stop playing church. The battle is real, and we are seeing fruits of that battle in North America in very real ways. The many swaths of Christianity that downplay this spiritual element have helped to foster an attitude of comfort and complacency in our spiritual walk—ailments that have seeped into the psyche of our Christian culture.

As a believer, this is where the battle becomes very significant. The devil wants nothing more than to make us irrelevant. There is nothing the devil wants more than to take away our joy, our testimony, or our ability to reach others for Christ. He cannot take away our eternal salvation, but he can take away our ability to help someone else find that eternal salvation. There are many Christians who have been put on the shelf, or taken out of the game altogether, because they bought into a lie from Satan.

In the meantime, our prayers are significant, not only for what they bring relationally between God and us, but also for what they potentially invite. This other dimension deserves our attention and our serious reflection. Much like a soldier who scans the horizon for any sign of an enemy that could potentially be lying in wait and poised to attack.

One more thought needs to be expressed here. To those who serve congregations around the world you are the front-line workers confronting the forces of evil. A sermon is not a thirty-minute speech, it is war. That is why, for many, it is such an exhausting experience because it is challenging the forces of evil head-on. It is why it is imperative for the preacher to be bathed in prayer, preparation, and piety. The same is true for the life of the church and why gatherings for prayer so critical. Communal prayer binds people together in communal warfare against the forces of darkness. It acknowledges the reality of the enemy, and the importance of prayer as a weapon of war.

6

DUPLICATE

ASK MOST PEOPLE WHAT prayer is, and the answer will likely be something like; *Prayer is simply talking to God*. I cannot begin to tell you the number of times I have heard that definition. It has been echoed by everyone from well-meaning conference speakers to people of little to no faith background.

In every case, I believe there is an honest attempt to demystify prayer, to remove some of the anxieties that come with any practice where people are unsure of how to engage it in the first place. After all, if you are going to address the almighty, there must certainly be some kind of protocol, right? Even on a human level, to be in the company of human royalty demands you follow certain guidelines when in the presence of a monarch.

To complicate matters further, prayer is, for many, a private matter. It is no secret that for most, getting up in front of a crowd is a daunting enterprise. Asking someone to pray in front of a crowd raises the anxiety level that much more.

The appeal of *simply talking to God* is also an attempt to reassure people that there is really no wrong way to go about praying. The ears of God are attentive to any and all who simply and sincerely lift their voices in petition to him, whether it's a child, a senior or anyone in between. If you can talk to a friend then, surely, you can just as easily talk to God. It would, therefore, stand to reason that a God who is compassionate and merciful is more interested in hearing the heart of our prayer, rather than correcting us on its form.

Many of us have never been taught how to pray. We either fumble until we find a comfort level, or mimic what we have heard or read from others. For those having had some kind of formal instruction on prayer, it is usually based on a prescribed formula or acronym, meant to prompt the various components of prayer that should ultimately come to mind.

Prayer formulas have their place as a teaching tool, especially for those who need some kind of mnemonic to help them in the discipline of prayer. Regardless, when we really consider the importance of prayer, engagement in the practice would naturally take precedence over its form, or lack thereof.

Therefore, is prayer simply talking to God? On one hand it is a fair statement to make. However, though it is meant to alleviate the anxiety many have about prayer, it does not convey the full biblical picture. All criticism aside, the desire to make the practice of prayer less intimidating is an admirable one, but if we are to be authentic in our practice of such an important discipline, it stands to reason that some guidelines are better than others. After all, we want our prayers to be effective do we not?

Cultural Shift

The culture of first-century Judaism had a long religious history by the time Jesus Christ entered the scene. Few nations could claim the religious legacy of the Jewish people, with its deep relationship to the Torah, Temple, and Mosaic Law with all its stipulations and ethical requirements. It was a nation birthed by an exodus from slavery through the miraculous hand of God, and established by a covenant with him.

Few nations, if any, could boast of such origins. Such beginnings came with a host of religious observances, sacrifices, and obligations that formed traditions and rituals that spanned centuries. Over time, nothing escaped the meticulous nature of the

Jewish scribes and rabbis. Every aspect of life was filtered through the religious lens of the Torah and given practical expression to be lived out on a daily basis.

We are told in the Talmud, a collection of writings for governing the civic life of the Jewish people, that during the First Temple period, prayer was entirely spontaneous. It was not until the Second Temple period that formalized prayer became necessary. This was due to the fact that people who were returning from Babylonian exile lacked both the language and the knowledge of Judaism.[1]

What followed was a system of prayer and benedictions that governed the formal services of the synagogues. It consisted of three opening benedictions, three closing benedictions, and twelve intermediary ones containing various requests. The opening benedictions honored the faith of the founding fathers, the power of the Almighty, the resurrection of the dead, and the holiness of God. The closing benedictions were for the restoration of worship in the Temple, a return of the Spirit of God, thanksgiving for life, and for peace in the world.[2]

The twelve intermediary prayers were for knowledge, repentance, forgiveness, redemption, healing of the sick, success of crops, ingathering of the exiles, righteous judgment, punishment of the wicked, reward for the pious, restoration of David's rule, and a final request that all supplications be answered.[3]

These eighteen benedictions as a whole are known as *Shemoneh Esreh*, or simply *Tefilah*, meaning prayer. Beyond these formal benedictions were fixed times that were also devoted to prayer, mostly corresponding to the public sacrifice ceremonies in the Temple. A prayer was recited at dawn, a second at the evening sacrifice, as well as an evening prayer not directly connected to a sacrifice. A third prayer was also instituted but was not given the kind of fixed requirements of the first two. Prayer services were

---

1. Steinsalz, *The Essential Talmud*, 101.
2. Steinsalz, *The Essential Talmud*, 102.
3. Steinsalz, *The Essential Talmud*, 102.

also augmented by the *Shema* "Hear, O Israel, the Lord our God, the Lord is One," from Deuteronomy 6:4-9; 11:13-21.

This is only a brief synopsis of the Jewish history and progression of prayer, but it is important to understand the cultural context of the passage that is the focus of this chapter. The prayer in question is the most commonly recited prayer from the Bible, and one for which volumes have been written over the centuries.

Teach Us to Pray

It is into the rich history of the Jewish people and their religious devotion, that Jesus enters. As he gathered his twelve disciples, he would spend the next few years pouring into them and preparing them for what lay ahead.

One of the most significant passages on the teachings of Jesus is known as the Sermon on the Mount, found in Matthew chapters 5-7. In this sermon, Jesus teaches on a wide range of topics, but for our purposes here, we will look at the section that deals specifically with prayer found in Matthew 6:5-6:14. The prayer portion of this section is most commonly known as The Lord's Prayer.

Though Matthew contains the section on prayer within the Sermon on the Mount, Luke presents it in his own unique context. In Luke chapter 11 we read the following: "Once Jesus was in a certain place praying. As he finished, one of his disciples came to him and said, "Lord, teach us to pray, just as John taught his disciples." (Luke 11:1).

Note that one of Jesus' disciples has asked Jesus to teach them how to pray. As innocent as that request may sound at first, it has important implications. For one, considering the background of the Jewish context, Jesus' disciples would have been steeped in the religious customs and expectations of Judaism. They would have been equally immersed in the prayer life of the community, if not the Synagogue itself. What is it that they see in Jesus that has not been part of their prayer experience that prompts such a question in the first place?

Secondly, the response from Jesus is quite telling. He does not respond with, "Simply talk to God." He actually gives them a model, or pattern, to emulate. Much has been written about the form of the prayer that Jesus teaches, but one has to wonder if part of the disciples' question was birthed due to the intimacy they saw in Jesus' prayers, as well as the results.

There is a third, equally fascinating thing to note. The disciple wants Jesus to teach them to pray, " . . . just as John taught his disciples." Not only did their experiences with Jesus challenge them about their prayer life, but it is something that John the Baptist has been teaching as well.

Historically, disciples of prominent rabbis would request that they be taught to pray which would distinguish them from other rabbinic schools.[4] Whatever the reason for the disciples' request of Jesus, something is being witnessed in Jesus' behavior that is a diversion from what they have typically seen or been taught.

The passage in Matthew does not have the initial question from the disciple, but it does have a longer preamble and prayer framework than Luke. The slight differences in the two versions are further evidence that Jesus has given us a model with key elements, rather than a word for word prayer demanding exact replication. Reciting this prayer is not functionally wrong, considering it serves as a powerful community expression. However, it appears to be given as a means of promoting a deeper prayer life through the giving of a pristine example.

A Model of Do's and Don'ts

As Jesus instructs his disciples on prayer, he begins with what they have experienced in the religious climate that they have grown up in. It is this cultural framework that has shaped the disciples' understanding of prayer. They would have likely learned the various prayers and benedictions as part of their upbringing that were

---

4. Steinsalz, *The Essential Talmud*, 102–4.

an integral part of their weekly synagogue attendance and temple worship.

During Jesus' Sermon on the Mount, he introduces the topic of prayer by first and foremost teaching what it is not.

> [5] "When you pray, don't be like the hypocrites who love to pray publicly on street corners and in the synagogues where everyone can see them. I tell you the truth, that is all the reward they will ever get. [6] But when you pray, go away by yourself, shut the door behind you, and pray to your Father in private. Then your Father, who sees everything, will reward you. [7] "When you pray, don't babble on and on as people of other religions do. They think their prayers are answered merely by repeating their words again and again. [8] Don't be like them, for your Father knows exactly what you need even before you ask him! (Matthew 6:5–8)

What is striking in this passage is the implication that the practice as presented by Jesus does not appear to be the rare or infrequent example. In teaching his disciples about prayer, and subsequently the assembled crowd that was also there, it is clear that he is addressing the practice that has become a platform for hypocrites. We get the word hypocrite from the Greek word for actor. Here were those who were deliberately using the times of public prayer to showcase their piety. To Jesus, it was nothing more than an act.

It would not be in keeping with Jesus to use an example that would be irrelevant to the crowd, so it is a telling indictment on the practice of prayer at the time. Practices that had been originated as vehicles for drawing people into a more intimate relationship with God are now being perverted for personal glory. The only benefit or reward they will gain for such acting is nothing more than superficial praise from others and a bloated sense of self-righteousness.

Prayer is not a system of chants or incantations, or a means by which one can charm God to do one's bidding. It is not a vehicle for manipulation or a marathon for demonstrating our piety to God and to others. Repetition has its place, in that it helps to reinforce a tradition or habit, but it can also dull the senses as to its original intent. We can become so familiar with patterns and words that they can quickly lose any meaning and any real connection or authenticity.

No passage raises the question, "What is the purpose of praying"? more than this passage. If prayer is a matter of locking myself away in private, and God knows what I need before I even ask him, then what is the sense of it all? No question points to the myopic understanding of prayer more than this, because it sees prayer only as a vehicle of transaction. This is treating prayer as nothing more than asking God for what I want. Otherwise, why bother praying?

In contrast to the hypocrites that Jesus mentions, he beautifully paints the heart of what authentic prayer looks like. It is the expression of an intimate relationship with God. In other words, it is the underlying attitude of faith that undergirds a proper prayer ethic. It is not seeking to get something out of God but to be in communion with him.

Further, this passage doesn't necessarily speak against liturgical forms or even against public or repetitive prayers. For one, Jesus in the next section actually presents a formulaic prayer, and secondly, Jesus himself prayed publicly and with repetition and length (See Matthew 6:9–13; 26:44; Luke 6:12; John 11:41–43). Jesus needed first and foremost to highlight the ways in which God's intention for prayer had become hijacked for spiritual showmanship.

A Paradigm Presented

With a clearer understanding of what constitutes authentic prayer and what does not, Jesus now presents a paradigm for his disciples to emulate:

> [9] Pray like this: Our Father in heaven, may your name be kept holy.
> [10] May your Kingdom come soon. May your will be done on earth, as it is in heaven.

¹¹ Give us today the food we need,
¹² and forgive us our sins, as we have forgiven those who sin against us.
¹³ And don't let us yield to temptation, but rescue us from the evil one. (Matthew 6:9–13)

Few prayers have garnered centuries of commentary as the one presented here. In a handful of verses, Jesus gives a broad overview of the essentials that constitute dynamic prayer. It can further be argued that the order of priorities is also of importance to note, but in its essence, the prayer is not so much a command, but an invitation to share in the prayer life of Jesus himself.⁵

What has been witnessed of Jesus is a prayer life that is intimate, authentic, dynamic, focused, purposeful, and effective. So much so, that it prompts the disciples' request to teach them (Luke 11:1), and causes the crowd at the end of the Sermon on the Mount to exclaim how Jesus taught with real authority, unlike the religious leaders (Matthew 7:28–29). Jesus is teaching a praying culture how to pray.

In terms of basic patterns, the prayer can be broken into two distinct sections. The first section (vss. 9–10) prioritizes the vertical relationship with God while the second section (vss. 11–13) prioritizes the horizontal realities and needs. Jesus places as primary importance the nature of our relationship with a God who is holy, and the need to align ourselves with God's will and purposes. Hence, a prayer that is focused on God's kingdom and priorities.

This is what is overwhelmingly missing from the majority of prayers. Part of the impetus for this book was the recognition that for the most part, prayers revolve around two primary dimensions, the personal and the community. The personal dimension is when we petition God for personal needs while the community one is the petitioning God for the needs of others.

The missing dimension is what we are calling the "kingdom" one. Here, in the paradigm presented by Jesus, it holds primacy over the personal and the community. It is God's kingdom we pray for, and, furthermore, that we experience his will on earth. As a

---

5. Wright, *Lord's Prayer as a Paradigm for Christian Prayer*, 132.

focal point, it orients our entire prayer life on the character and nature of God, and on his plan and purposes first and foremost.

From there, Jesus moves to the horizontal needs (the personal and community), and stresses our reliance and dependency on God for our daily needs, as well as the necessity of spiritual health and vitality. This should not go unnoticed. The only physical need that is asked in this prayer is the one for daily sustenance.

In one short paradigm, Jesus has framed prayer with the following key essentials. First, the primacy of a relationship with God who is at once our Father as well as holy. The Jews at the time would have likely bristled at the intimate nature of claiming God as "our Father." Though the prayer that Jesus presents is beyond the comfort level of the prevailing culture, it is still steeped with a sense of worship, reverence, and awe.

Secondly, Jesus reminds us that God has a plan and purpose for the world we live in. A will and a kingdom that mimics the heavenly realm. From there, Jesus presents the necessity of daily dependence on God, framed through the basic need of daily bread. The need for dependence on God is further illustrated by the appeal for forgiveness, here given in the full scope of its theological import. We also see forgiveness from God for the sins we commit, and the reciprocal act of forgiving others as a result of our being forgiven.

Lastly, beyond the acknowledgement of our sin and the weight it imposes on the soul, is the recognition of the darkness that lurks because of the evil one himself—the Devil, Satan, the Deceiver. As noted in the previous chapter, we exist in a spiritual war zone, and no one would understand its real-world impact more than Jesus.

Prayer Reorientation

In many ways, what has been dubbed, The Lord's Prayer, is a prayer of reorientation (especially for the original disciples), rooted in the intimate and relational aspect of God. As Jesus begins to teach his disciples how to pray, he first teaches them what they should not mimic when it comes to authentic prayer, while at the same time reorienting them to a model of prayer that reflects God's original intent.

The prayer that Jesus presents here can also serve as a filter for evaluating our own prayer lives. By asking a series of questions we can quickly determine whether our prayer life is aligned with the model that Jesus presents to the disciples. In fact, these same questions can even serve as a litmus test for your overall spiritual life.

First, we need to ask ourselves, "Where is my focus"? Is it on building intimacy with God as our Heavenly Father and do we live in reverence of his character and nature? Secondly, "What are my priorities"? When we pray, do we truly long for God's will to be done on earth? Thirdly, "What is my motivation"? Are we asking God for what we want versus what we need and is our prayer acknowledging a daily dependence on him?

Our tendency towards self-reliance can often come at the expense of recognizing the importance of daily reliance on God for our deepest needs. Fourthly, "What is the condition of my heart"? Do we recognize the forgiveness and grace that has been extended to us, and do we live a life of forgiveness and grace extended to others? Lastly, "Where do I look for help"? Do we acknowledge the spiritual battle that exists, and do we seek the Lord's deliverance, or do we simply try to manage the battle in our own strength and abilities? These are simple questions, but they can unlock a host of potential spiritual pitfalls.

If we truly want to touch the heart of God, it is not with theatrics, glory-seeking, or even eloquence of speech. Jesus stated that prayer was more about relationship than mere words or requests. But relationships take work, especially if they are to remain healthy and vibrant over time. It is much easier to forgo the work and move into request mode, because, after all, that is why most of us bother with prayer in the first place.

It is easy to pray like a hypocrite. It is much harder to pray in the manner of Jesus. In the former, you receive the reward that a hypocrite deserves, but in the latter, you will have deeper communion with the living God. This takes praying with humility, with the intent of honoring God, but the reward is well worth the effort.

I have only focused on specific verses related to the topic of prayer but if you read further into chapter 6, from verses 14 to 18, Jesus warns against having a heart of unforgiveness, and then repeats the teaching pattern for fasting that he has just given for prayer. Do not be like the hypocrites who present themselves in a disheveled manner when they fast. Contrary to them, fast in private but in public look well-groomed and presentable. It is the concluding statement to the entire section on prayer and fasting that deserves our attention. It is found in verse 18b: "And your Father, who sees everything, will reward you."

The contrast that Jesus presents between the hypocrites and the model he taught his disciples is an interesting one. The rewards that the hypocrites receive, whether in prayer or fasting, are easily determined by the acts themselves. These important spiritual disciplines are for their own personal glorification.

To those who follow the authentic model that Jesus presents there is also a reward, one that is given by our heavenly father. What is not clarified is what that reward entails. What this potential reward could possibly be is not defined or even hinted at. If one looks to the specific context, it could be argued that the reward is a deepening relationship with God.

Arguably, this may be Jesus' entire point in this section of the Sermon on the Mount (6:5-18). Over the practices of the religious hypocrites comes instructions on how we can build an authentic relationship with God, one where our hearts become aligned with his. Through that relationship, we experience life as God intended. As with any relationship that has been nurtured through time, and weathered through both good seasons and bad, the rewards of such a relationship are far too numerous to list.

Jesus is advocating for a prayer life infused by a relational intent that sees God as much more than a giver of good gifts. He is also a friend who knows us more intimately than we know ourselves and is now desiring for us to know him more completely.

Such relationships foster a depth and vibrancy of faith that cannot be compared to expressions of superficial religiosity. In this one simple model of prayer, Jesus gives us all we need to deepen not only our prayer life but also our entire spiritual life.

7

Alignment

In determining the biblical prayers that would serve the intent of this book, the passage that will be the focus of this particular chapter is one of the most important prayers in all of Scripture. Not only because of the context that we find the prayer, but because of the challenge it presents to not only the modern church, but the church throughout the ages.

At the time of this writing, the world has been experiencing a global pandemic in Covid-19. We have been in a constant cycle of lockdowns of various degrees and nothing in recent memory has challenged our social, economic, and cultural ways of life as this viral onslaught. As much as I wanted to leave the matter of the pandemic out of this writing, it serves as a key illustration for what will be discussed in this chapter.

When the threat of the pandemic became evident, one of the first reactions from most governments around the world was to stop public gatherings and limit personal contact. This had huge implications for the church because, after all, we are practically defined by our gatherings. Churches, virtually overnight, could no longer conduct public services, something that we have taken for granted for centuries.

In order to remain connected to their congregations and to remain viable, churches now had to find new ways of gathering, primarily through virtual services and online platforms. Many churches were already occupying that space, so it was an easy transition, but for some the hesitancy to move into that space prior to Covid left them at a severe disadvantage.

Churches, regardless of whether or not they could transition to the new reality, all faced the same dilemma. Can we still be the church even though we are not physically meeting together? It was a difficult time, not only for churches, but for whole industries and small businesses whose livelihood was now in peril. The church, by comparison, fared better than many businesses, both large and small, that could not weather the long-term closure of their shops.

In times of difficulty, the values, character, and strength of an organization come to the forefront. The same is true for the church, and when the pandemic hit, the expectation was that it would become an opportunity for the church to shine. After all, is the church not a haven from the difficulties and inconsistencies of life?

When the Going Gets Tough . . .

At a time when the church should have had its moment to show the rest of the world the reason it exists, we found some who turned the opportunity into a political and cultural fiasco. From conspiracy theories to outright defiance, churches were being featured in the media in ways that were less than complimentary. At a time when most were trying to manage a serious health crisis, some churches were doing very little to advance the biblical dictum of "loving your neighbor."

Most ironic is the fact that for the first time in recent memory, the culture at large was responding to a health crisis in a more christian way than expected. Normally, the health concerns of the population do not necessarily take precedence over the all mighty dollar. However, in this case, health was the primary concern.

All this is not to say that there was wholesale agreement on how this pandemic was managed or how various governments fared in protecting their populations. The disappointment for many was how the church was seen in light of the situation. From the vantage point of the non-churched, the church was seen as protecting its own rights and its own authority to govern itself. All theological arguments aside, when those you desire to reach see you as self-serving and uncaring of the larger community, then any chance of reaching them quickly dissolves.

Mind you, the vast majority of churches demonstrated being the hands and feet of Jesus during this difficult time yet, as with all things related in the world of media consumption, the extreme stories get the most airtime. This season has exposed one of the glaring discrepancies within the church, one that has never been fully resolved and continues to divide us further. It is also one of the more compelling arguments given for those who are non-churched or critical of the church as to why they could not be bothered with it.

Before we get to the heart of what is being argued in this chapter a final point needs to be stressed. Due to this apparent discrepancy in the church, an unfavorable caricature of the church and Jesus is presented. This is most concerning. There are many who reject the Church, Jesus Christ, God, the Holy Spirit, and the Bible, based not on authentic understanding of such important matters, but on caricatures and misguided examples. It is one thing to reject the message of Jesus, it is another thing altogether to reject a distortion.

A Timeless Prayer

As the pandemic continued to wreak havoc and the response of some churches continued to take center stage, one passage would come to mind time and again. A crisis like the Covid pandemic illustrates the power of this prayer as well as the desperate need for its fulfilment. It comes from the Gospel of John and is known as the High Priestly Prayer of Jesus that is found in chapter 17.

In terms of timelines, this appears to be one of the final prayers of Jesus we have recorded prior to his crucifixion, the final one being his prayer in Gethsemane as found in Matthew 26:36–46,

Mark 14:32-42, and Luke 22:39-46. If it is indeed one of his final petitions, then it would stand to reason that it serves as a marker of the important issues that lay heavy on the heart of Jesus. It can in some ways be seen as a type of final will, a closing epitaph for all he wanted to leave as final instructions before going to the cross.

The prayer in its full form is presented below, and it is worthy of reading in its entirety.

> [1] After saying all these things, Jesus looked up to heaven and said, "Father, the hour has come. Glorify your Son so he can give glory back to you. [2] For you have given him authority over everyone. He gives eternal life to each one you have given him. [3] And this is the way to have eternal life—to know you, the only true God, and Jesus Christ, the one you sent to earth. [4] I brought glory to you here on earth by completing the work you gave me to do. [5] Now, Father, bring me into the glory we shared before the world began.
>
> [6] "I have revealed you to the ones you gave me from this world. They were always yours. You gave them to me, and they have kept your word. [7] Now they know that everything I have is a gift from you, [8] for I have passed on to them the message you gave me. They accepted it and know that I came from you, and they believe you sent me.
>
> [9] "My prayer is not for the world, but for those you have given me, because they belong to you. [10] All who are mine belong to you, and you have given them to me, so they bring me glory. [11] Now I am departing from the world; they are staying in this world, but I am coming to you. Holy Father, you have given me your name; now protect them by the power of your name so that they will be united just as we are. [12] During my time here, I protected them by the power of the name you gave me. I guarded them so that not one was lost, except the one headed for destruction, as the Scriptures foretold.
>
> [13] "Now I am coming to you. I told them many things while I was with them in this world so they would be filled with my joy. [14] I have given them your word. And the world hates them because they do not belong

to the world, just as I do not belong to the world. [15] I'm not asking you to take them out of the world, but to keep them safe from the evil one. [16] They do not belong to this world any more than I do. [17] Make them holy by your truth; teach them your word, which is truth. [18] Just as you sent me into the world, I am sending them into the world. [19] And I give myself as a holy sacrifice for them so they can be made holy by your truth.

[20] "I am praying not only for these disciples but also for all who will ever believe in me through their message. [21] I pray that they will all be one, just as you and I are one—as you are in me, Father, and I am in you. And may they be in us so that the world will believe you sent me.

[22] "I have given them the glory you gave me, so they may be one as we are one. [23] I am in them and you are in me. May they experience such perfect unity that the world will know that you sent me and that you love them as much as you love me. [24] Father, I want these whom you have given me to be with me where I am. Then they can see all the glory you gave me because you loved me even before the world began!

[25] "O righteous Father, the world doesn't know you, but I do; and these disciples know you sent me. [26] I have revealed you to them, and I will continue to do so. Then your love for me will be in them, and I will be in them." (John 17:1–26)

The richness of this prayer cannot be overstated. The intimacy of the Upper Room with his disciples will soon transition to a garden in the Kidron Valley and the subsequent arrest of Jesus, leading to his crucifixion. The prayer found here illustrates the matters that weigh on Jesus' heart as he prepares to offer his life as a sacrifice for the sins of the world. Salvation is a costly gift.

The prayer is typically outlined in the following way. First, Jesus prays for his glorification (vss. 1–5). For Jesus to be glorified is to also glorify the Father who sent him. This section is unique in that it is one of those rare moments when Jesus is focused on himself (other instances where we see this are the Transfiguration, Matthew 17:1–9, the Triumphal Entry, Mark 1:1–11, and the prayer in Gethsemane, Luke 22:39–46). These moments when Jesus allows the recognition of the crowd or the petition of his prayers on himself are important transitions, especially in the final week of his life.

To state that Jesus is focused on himself is a bit misleading in that his prayer seeks the glory of the Father through the son, Jesus. The bond between the two cannot be denied. Though the Holy Spirit is not specifically mentioned in this prayer, he has been prominent in the larger context of the Upper Room discourse. The trinitarian undertones of Jesus' prayer will become the foundational grid for the remainder of the prayer, especially in the latter section that will be the center of our focus.

The second part of the prayer (vss. 6–19) concerns the disciples. The intimacy inferred from the first five verses between the Father and the Son is now intimated to the disciples of Jesus. These are the twelve in whom he has poured his life, in preparation for his departure and for the mission he has entrusted to them. Here, Jesus prays for their protection and sanctification. They will face the hostility and hatred of the world because of the message they will proclaim, a message of truth and hope that will be countered by the evil one. Despite what they will face, Jesus prays that they will experience joy and holiness, now that they have been exposed to the truth. As Jesus prepares to leave them, he prays for the days that they will face as they take the message of Jesus to the world.

The Church's Greatest Challenge

The last section of the prayer, found in verses 20–26, is the section that is of particular interest for our purposes. Here, Jesus prays for all future disciples—in other words, the church. It is striking to realize that as a believer, Jesus has prayed for us. As with the previous sections of this prayer, the theme of the oneness shared by the Father and Son would be a hallmark of not only the disciples who walked with Jesus, but all future disciples as well.

Herein lies the greatest challenge the church has ever faced and the most consistent problem throughout the centuries—the problem of unity. The history of the church is one that is replete with divisions, disagreements, splits, and outright war. This does not include the multiple battles that the church has waged externally with the culture, but the internal ones that continue to cause it to implode.

Jesus' concern for unity is critical, not only for what it does for the harmony of the believing body, but also for the way it will serve as a witness to the validity of the gospel message. What cannot be denied is that the unity which Jesus prays for is something that should be observable by the world. Instead of the church being known for what it is against, it should be noted more for demonstrating the character of Christ.

Earlier in John's Gospel, Jesus gave his disciples a new commandment, found in John 13:34: "So now I am giving you a new commandment: Love each other. Just as I have loved you, you should love each other." Jesus, who had come and fulfilled the tenets and the purpose of the Old Testament Law (Matthew 5:17), replaces them with this single but most difficult of commands—to love. This forms the backdrop of Jesus' prayer for unity.

No command is more difficult to obey than the command to love. Even though love is the single common need of every human who has ever lived, it is the one emotion we humans continually wrestle with. If we were to recall the happiest moment of our lives as well as the most difficult, love would likely be the common denominator between the two. Because love can be so volatile it can quickly turn toxic and can make the most rational person react in childish fits.

When we are starved for love, we can quickly move into survival mode and will break our own moral and ethical codes in order to feed our starvation. Even when applied to the theology of God, love is either the most doubted aspect of his character or the most affirmed, both of which in their treatment present a narrow caricature of God. For those who have experienced a life event that challenges the notion of a loving God, they cannot reconcile that aspect of his character based on their experience. At the other extreme is the God of love who does not judge or even discipline, and holds no one accountable.

Jesus' command to love is not only the greatest challenge for the church, because it is at the core of his prayer for unity, but is also the greatest challenge for believers individually. The most courageous thing you can do in your life is not to climb Everest, or to scale the face of El Capitan without a rope, but to love as Jesus loved. To fully live out the commandment of love is to recognize love in terms of sacrificial, unconditional, and transformational living. It is seeking the betterment of others, in a way to lift them up, not tear them down. I am not sure that the world has ever experienced a church that has lived out this principal command as Jesus demonstrated. The early church seems to have come closest, but since then, it has been a struggle for the universal church.

Why is love so hard? Because love can demand more from us than we are willing to give. Not everyone deserves to be loved, at least in our own minds. What of those who have hurt us? Love leaves emotional scars that are virtually impossible to erase. Scars can be powerful lessons but at the same time can also leave us hurt and unwilling to ever be vulnerable again. People who have been hurt build walls, and walls have a way of closing people off from certain influences. If the church is a reason for the wall's existence in the first place, the message of Jesus will have difficulty getting through. Truth is most appealing and most acceptable when done through acts of love, humility, and sacrifice. Even though it would be easy for the church to simply disengage from the culture around us, and validate our decision by claiming its hostility towards us, the church does not have the luxury of doing so.

The Tension is Real

The tensions raised by the question of unity are many. It is easy to spell out the deficiencies of the church in respect to unity but it is another thing altogether to put that unity into practice. What are the key doctrinal issues that demand agreement? What roles, functions, or ordinances authenticate a viable church? When does a church or individual no longer qualify for inclusion? What are the shared goals of the mission that the church has been given? Is it not the responsibility of the church to contend for the faith once delivered to the saints?

There is no doubt that the weight of this prayer continues to reveal the failure of the church to place unity as a priority in its practices and mission. Oftentimes, we are so concerned with the internal affairs of the church that we can neglect the greater witness of its actions. The parsing of our doctrinal statements and the administrative oversight of the church can dominate the focus of our gatherings. These are all important functions no doubt, but when they consume us to the degree that they distort the essence of what Jesus prays for, we have lost the heart of his prayer.

Despite the tensions that exist, the prayer for unity by Jesus cannot be ignored. Could it be said that one of the reasons for the church's struggle in reaching its culture is directly related to its inability to appear unified? As difficult as the question of unity is, the lingering effects of its lack are far reaching. So much so, that Jesus recognizes that without it, the world will struggle with believing in the mission and message of Jesus. If this was a part of one of Jesus' final prayers, would it not stand to reason that it should become part of our own prayer life? Could it not be understood as a prayer reminiscent of Matthew 6:10 where God's will would be seen on earth as it is in heaven?

It is this particular issue of unity that struck such a discordant note during the Covid-19 pandemic. Disagreements on so many levels abound during major, world-altering events, but the role of some churches who were more concerned about their own rights under the guise of religious freedom and the authority of Christ over the government smacked against the heart of Jesus' prayer in John 17.

Don't misunderstand the essence of what is being said. Conflicts and disagreements will always exist. It is basic to being human. The same is true in churches. The issue is when our differences are on display far more than our unified call and responsibility to be a witness to the world. At a time when people were feeling threatened economically, socially, and personally, some churches that gained the majority of media attention, portrayed the church as being uncaring to the community at large, even though they would argue otherwise.

Thankfully, many churches quietly continued to stay the course, and used this season as a means for touching lives. They demonstrated a heart of servitude and a sense of unity that spoke loudly to the communities in which they exist. Many believers stood with their neighbors and redefined the church by reminding their communities that it is the people, not the building who make up the church.

The church is not an institution for perfect people. It is a sanctuary for sinners saved by grace, empowered by the Holy Spirit to be the presence of Christ in a dark world. Its proclamation is the Gospel through the mandate of love. It is the bride of Christ, beautiful and radiant in its glory, where the children of God are nurtured for growth. It exists as a haven of hope and the guardian of truth, a defender of the helpless, and a refuge for broken souls. Though it is continually attacked, vilified, and criticized, it is the greatest hope for transforming our world.

Jesus, centuries ago, prayed for something that continues to be a struggle to this day and a constant barrier to the church's effectiveness in a rapidly changing world. There are also no easy solutions and while none have been offered here, one thing can be stated. The matter of unity is so mired in potential landmines due to our human limitations; it would take a movement of the Lord to bring about, even remotely, a unity that would speak to the non-believing world. Does it not stand to reason then that one way we can become more effective is to commit ourselves to pray for unity? A unity that does not devalue or depreciate the distinctives of our churches, but a unity of love that radiates the heart and message of Jesus Christ.

8

Knocking on Heaven's Door

Expectations are a big part of life. In their basic form, they are defined as a belief of what may happen in a particular scenario or situation. If we are not careful, our expectations can leave us feeling disillusioned and discouraged. Expectations that are high or unreasonable are most likely to leave us on the negative side of the equation. Conversely, to have our expectations exceeded is always a surprising and encouraging experience.

Expectations are a key component for goal setting. It is a way of projecting what can motivate and push us beyond our present limitations. In a completely self-centric world, the power of expectations is seen as a means of subconsciously controlling your life to fulfill the dreams you have always imagined. In the present self-help climate of advocating for more self-awareness, the ability to navigate our expectations, both positively and negatively, is seen as personal advancement and growth.

The better we are able to manage our expectations, the better we will be able to manage the times we are let down by others. To clarify expectations is a healthy tool to have in our relational toolbox. In every organization people have expectations, and without clarity, they will develop their own, whether or not they align with those of the organization. Ask an engaged couple what their expectations of marriage are, and you will likely hear some interesting answers. Not only that, but you will surely find a framework to begin counselling them.

Expectations are a big part of our spiritual lives as well. As much as we may not admit it, many of us have expectations of God, and they often run contrary to what Scripture portrays. In fact, one reason unbelievers have for not believing in God is often based on their expectations. They ask, "Why did God allow such a bad thing to happen," or wonder, "Why would a loving God judge anyone"? Their expectations are part of the false narrative and caricature that was addressed in the previous chapter.

Few of us, though, can escape the pull of expectations. After all, we do expect God to act, respond, and, most importantly, answer our prayers as part of our relationship with him. Often our expectations can venture from what could happen to what should happen. Though it is naturally human to have expectations, they can undoubtedly lead to trouble and confusion.

We see this in the New Testament when Jesus confronted the expectations of the religious leaders, especially as it concerned their ideas of the Messiah. For some, their expectations were of a messianic king, in keeping with the lineage and glory of David, Israel's most successful warrior king (Amos 9:11; Hosea 3:4–5; Isaiah 9:7). For others, they expected a human coming on the clouds, with power and authority, where every tribe and nation would serve him, and his kingdom would last forever and never be destroyed (Daniel 7:13–14). Few expected Jesus to live out the portrait of the suffering servant of Isaiah 53, a picture far removed from the popular notion of a Messiah at the time.

Releasing Our Expectations

Expectations can lead us into a number of different scenarios, both positive and negative. They can motivate us to better outcomes or fuel our worst fears. They can also wreak havoc with our prayer lives. We do not control the outcome of our prayers, only the shape of their presentation. In fairness, though, Jesus, as recorded in Mark's gospel, stated the following: "I tell you the truth, you can say to this mountain, 'May you be lifted up and thrown into the sea,' and it will happen. But you must really believe it will happen and have no doubt in your heart." (Mark 11:23; see also Mathew 21:21).

Jesus was citing a common rabbinic metaphor of uprooting mountains to describe faith, which is the basic condition for all our relationship with God. The expectation to move the mountain in this case is not on the person praying, but on the will and faithfulness of God to perform the miracle. In other ways, the statement by Jesus can also illustrate the duality of faith and doubt in moments of divine necessity. The context of unwavering faith in divine help prompts the potential for miracle, rooted in the faithfulness of God. Despite encouragement to the contrary, expectations can shape our prayers, even before we offer them.

Regardless, few of us ever pray without some kind of expectation regarding the outcome. And the more personal and emotionally charged the request, the greater likelihood of attaching expectations on how God should answer. There are even times when our expectations can be so defined that God may answer in such a way that we do not even recognize how God is working. We are looking in one direction, or for a particular outcome, while God may be doing something completely new, or in a totally opposite direction.

We also cannot ignore the way our life experiences shape our expectations when it comes to prayer. How many times have we heard someone tell us they are praying for a miracle, one that in the physical realm would break every law of nature and physics combined? Though we agree to partner in the need to pray, our inner spirit is battling between the tension of doubt and faith.

I recall early in ministry being at the bedside of an elderly person, one whom the doctors had clearly stated was in the last stages of life and for whom it was only a matter of hours. The doctors' encouragement to me was to give the person comfort and assurance in their final moments. As I settled by their bedside, the conversation soon turned to asking me to pray for them. To my surprise, they wanted me to ask God for a full recovery and healing. In fact, they asked me to pray that they would be able to resume life in a better physical state than they had been in many years.

Though I complied with the request, the tension I felt inside was palpable. As predicted by the doctors, the person was gone shortly after that fateful prayer. Was I being insincere and did my doubt make the prayer null and void? Was I simply putting on a brave face to help another transition from this life into the next? In those early experiences I found myself asking similar questions on a number of occasions.

As well-intentioned as our expectations may be, they do set us up for potential problems—especially as they relate to prayer. It is one thing to wrestle through the implications of our expectations in the normal routines of life, but with respect to prayer, our expectations can set the stage for disappointment, especially with God.

One of the more difficult disciplines to master is to release our prayers without expectations and to fully trust God with the outcome, no matter what it may be. Not only is that difficult, but accepting the answer in the full confidence and assurance of God's faithful love towards us can be equally challenging.

Expecting the Worse

In this particular section we are looking at a story that not only has some moments of comic relief, but also reminds us of the way expectations can act against our better intentions. We find it in the twelfth chapter of the Book of Acts. The chapter opens with Herod Agrippa actively persecuting the church, and has had the apostle James, the brother of the apostle John, killed with a sword.

This is the first indication of persecution by the Roman authorities against the church and by all accounts the Jewish people are pleased by the actions of Herod. Herod takes advantage of the political favor it has garnered him and also arrests the apostle, Peter. We are told this takes place during the celebration of the Passover which means the city of Jerusalem would have been crowded due to the many pilgrims there for the festivities. There is irony in this celebration that commemorated the deliverance of God, yet is now the backdrop for the unfolding of this chapter. The persecution that now ensues is motivated by nothing more than political gain, with prominent believers as the target.

As Peter is thrown into prison, there are two contrasts that are stressed in the text as found in vss. 4–6. Four squads of four soldiers each, that is sixteen soldiers, are guarding Peter. As if that was not enough, he is chained by both hands between two of them. Under the circumstances, escape was considered impossible. To the opposite extreme, we are also told that the church was praying fervently for Peter. The believers in this story did the only thing they could do in dire circumstances, and that is pray. When hopeless situations arise, the most hopeful thing we can do is pray. What would have driven others to despair drove the church to its knees.

We take up the story starting in verse 7:

> [7] Suddenly, there was a bright light in the cell, and an angel of the Lord stood before Peter. The angel struck him on the side to awaken him and said, "Quick! Get up!" And the chains fell off his wrists. [8] Then the angel told him, "Get dressed and put on your sandals." And he did. "Now put on your coat and follow me," the angel ordered.
> [9] So Peter left the cell, following the angel. But all the time he thought it was a vision. He didn't realize it was actually happening. [10] They passed the first and second guard posts and came to the iron gate leading to the city, and this opened for them all by itself. So they passed through and started walking down the street, and then the angel suddenly left him. [11] Peter finally came to his senses. "It's really true!" he said. "The Lord has sent his angel and saved me from Herod and from what the Jewish leaders had planned to do to me!" (Acts 12:7–11)

There is a hint of Greek humor in the text as an angel is sent to free Peter from the prison. Despite being scheduled for execution, Peter is sleeping soundly, and needs the prodding of the angel to awake him from his slumber. The angel's coaching amidst the grogginess of Peter is a further comedic touch and finally Peter comes to his senses allowing the angel to lead him in safety away from the prison. Our story continues in verse 12:

> [12] When he realized this, he went to the home of Mary, the mother of John Mark, where many were gathered for prayer. [13] He knocked at the door in the gate, and a servant girl named Rhoda came to open it. [14] When she recognized Peter's voice, she was so overjoyed that, instead of opening the door, she ran back inside and told everyone, "Peter is standing at the door!" [15] "You're out of your mind!" they said. When she insisted, they decided, "It must be his angel." [16] Meanwhile, Peter continued knocking. When they finally opened the door and saw him, they were amazed. [17] He motioned for them to quiet down and told them how the Lord had led him out of prison. "Tell James and the other brothers what happened," he said. And then he went to another place.
> [18] At dawn there was a great commotion among the soldiers about what had happened to Peter. [19] Herod Agrippa ordered a thorough search for him. When he couldn't be found, Herod interrogated the guards and sentenced them to death. Afterward Herod left Judea to stay in Caesarea for a while. (Act 12:12-19)

As soon as Peter realizes he is free, he makes for the home of Mary, where many were gathered for prayer. The arrival of Peter to the home is one of the more encouraging stories because of the honest human element that is on display. This story has not been sanitized or given the saintly treatment in that the arrival of Peter serves as a shock to the praying community.

Rhoda is forever memorialized in the pages of the Bible for her role in the story. Her own shock at Peter's arrival is met with an even larger one from the gathered crowd. This pronouncement that Peter is at the door is met with insults hurled at Rhoda who is accused of being out of her mind or confusing Peter with his angel. As they press the young servant girl, Peter continues to knock, until finally the door is opened, and all are left amazed.

The skeptic in me can look at the story and wonder why the very people who are praying for Peter are surprised when he actually shows up. Even the eyewitness of the young servant girl, Rhoda, is met with incredulity. She could not have seen the actual apostle, they reason, the answer to their prayers must have been some kind of mistake or illusion. Though those praying in the room would likely never admit it, their response tends to indicate that they had already written Peter off. After all, he was surrounded and bound by a multitude of Roman soldiers, men highly trained and efficient in their duties. To write Peter off is essentially to write God off. But God had other plans.

How One Expectation Leads to Another

We are in the realm of miracle as we recount the story of Peter's angelic rescue from the prison. Remember that the chapter began with the murder of the apostle James. In a single chapter we see one apostle lose his life while another experiences a miraculous escape. As the church community was reeling from the loss of one of their beloved apostles, another apostle was being lined up for execution, and from all reasonable expectations, the pattern would just repeat itself until the church was erased.

We all long to pray with hopeful anticipation. I am personally encouraged that the early believers in this story are open about their amazement as they witness Peter standing alive and in person in their doorway. What they had just experienced with the execution of James was a pattern of events they could easily see repeated. Based on what happened to James, is it any wonder that they would expect the same fate for Peter? Why did God protect one apostle but not the other? Whether we want to admit it or not, we can pray with hope while at the same time struggle with doubt.

What is of further encouragement is that this story comes at a time when the early church was witnessing miracles, signs, and wonders. It was a time when the Spirit of God and the power of God were taking the world by storm. Stories were coming in on a daily basis of lives being transformed and whole cultures having to meet the challenge of the ever-growing church. Many of us look back to that period in the history of the church with longing, praying that we would once again see the world-changing phenomena of the first-century, even though it may be more nostalgia generated than factual.

Prayer is that incredible dynamic whereby we experience all the ups and downs of faith. There are times where we are left wondering why our prayers seem to fall on deaf ears while others are answered so dramatically that they make us rub our eyes in disbelief. We spoke about the tension between "Can he"? and "Will he"? in an earlier chapter. There is no easy answer as to why one prayer is answered while another one is not, only to say that you are never done until God says you are done.

We love to believe that we are in control. We can plan, prioritize, strategize, invest, and so much more, but control and outcome belong to God. We do not control the outcome of our prayers, that is one thing for sure, but we certainly posit our expectations as to the answers. But the heart of faith is trusting in God's outcome—his decisions and actions—whatever that may be, because faith and trust go hand in hand. Whenever we determine how our prayers should be answered, we lose out on the wonder of God's answer.

Our expectations in some way reflect an attempt to take control of the outcome, however well-intentioned they may be. It is a subtle attempt to take the results out of God's hands and put them back into ours. It is one reason why doubt, when fueled by our expectations, is something that Jesus himself recognized as a barrier to authentic faith. Though there are times we claim to have faith in God, we can often be hesitant in trusting him fully with our lives.

To revisit an earlier point, expectations can lead to a sense of disappointment with God. How many people have stated how God had let them down or left them in a difficult situation? Have we ever questioned why God allows us to languish in our present circumstances? Maybe there is something redeeming in the present that is being missed because our expectations are causing us to look and hope elsewhere.

Striking in the stories of James and Peter is the apparent silence related to the way God responds to both situations. For the Biblical writers there is no contradiction or question concerning the character of God, or why he chooses to act in one situation and not in another. What is tragic for one is divine intervention for the other. There is frankly no interrogation or questioning by those in the story as to what God was thinking? Both are accepted as part of the realities of living in a fallen world. For reasons known only to God, Peter still had purpose in God's plan.

Warning, Expectations Dead Ahead

Expectations are implicit expressions of our convictions and personal beliefs, even though we may not recognize them as such. Hence their power of persuasion and why we can become so unnerved when they are not met. We can easily mistake an expectation where we thought something should have happened but did not, and assume that something must be wrong with our relationship with God. Even worse, we can assume that something must be wrong with God. Rarely would we consider our expectations to be misguided, especially when we find God's response unacceptable.

Expectations can serve as a kind of litmus test. They can gauge whether or not we view God in healthy ways. An unhealthy expectation would see God as cavalier and uncaring about the affairs of his creation, and even blame him directly for the injustices in the world, whereas a healthy one would lean more into his love and grace. Whether it is a healthy or unhealthy expectation, it can shape the way we respond to God in prayer.

Expectations can also be clues to the blind areas of our lives—those areas where assumptions rule, or our preferences, or what we believe is right over wrong, more than the reality. We can hold so tightly to a version of God that we can ignore anything that does not square with our concepts. This is why theological and doctrinal grounding in Scripture is so important. It helps us to understand the revealed character and nature of God so that theology rules and not our expectations. Besides, as God, he is free to act however he sees fit. As disturbing as you may find it, he is not answerable to us.

This is not to say that we cannot pray expectantly, or without confidence in God to answer, but it does serve as a warning that the answer is ultimately up to God, not us. We can become so tainted by life and the way that it drives our expectations that we place such demands on God that we can miss what he is actually accomplishing in our lives. How often do we ask God to rid us of a problem when God would rather walk us through a problem in order to teach us something that we would otherwise never learn? God is more interested in growing us and in who we are becoming than where we are going. Even our circumstances are used by God to shape and grow our faith.

Does this mean God never rescues or saves us? Of course not. God has proven many times over that he specializes in surprising us in ways unimaginable. There are those glorious moments when God exceeds our expectations, our faith is lifted, and our confidence in God restored. Our ability to set aside our expectations is a way of releasing ourselves into the providential hands of God. To pray and to solemnly declare that it is now in the Lord's hands and that "his will be done," is a discipline that will mark our prayer lives in significant ways.

9

Communication Breakdown

It was early evening and darkness had already descended as the church met for its weekly prayer meeting. At the time, I was a leader in a youth group that was on a mission trip to give help to this church. As part of their thanking us, they invited us to join them at their weekly meeting. There was a sense of urgency that revolved around some significant things God was doing in the midst of this church, so the meeting had an air of heightened anticipation.

As the people assembled, the room soon filled to capacity. What was truly encouraging was the number of families that made up the majority of those in attendance. Most prayer meetings lack the youth element, but here were young children gathered with their parents as part of a dedicated service of prayer to acknowledge and give thanks to the Lord.

As the evening progressed, the realization that I was part of something significant and memorable quickly became apparent. When the invitation for anyone to pray was made available, I witnessed family after family stand up and pray with such heart and passion that it touched my soul in a way that few moments have since.

The reason this particular evening is burned into my memory is that throughout the entire prayer meeting, I did not understand a single word of what was being said. I was in a non-English context, and I could not speak the language that governed this particular meeting. I was a spectator at best, and beyond the few words at the beginning of the meeting that were translated for me, the rest of the evening was entirely in a foreign tongue.

You would think such a setting would have left me uncomfortable and bored, especially since the meeting lasted about two hours. But it was one of the most moving nights of my life. What was truly inspiring was the number of young children who stood up and prayed before a crowd that would have intimidated so many others. I witnessed six-year old's, teenagers, and youth across the age spectrum give beautiful and heartfelt petitions that stirred the hearts of everyone in the room.

If there is an inherent intimidation to praying in public, the memo seems to have missed this group. No one, whether child or adult, appeared to be intimidated by public prayer. Though I could not understand a word, I sensed the weight of the Spirit of God within the room. Every human heart was joined together in a unity and a oneness that I can barely comprehend to this day. It was a beautiful example to me of heartfelt prayer and worship, and what happens in those moments when what we say becomes less important than how we say it.

When Words Fail

Words can sometimes fall short of what needs to be said. There are moments when words fail to express what the heart is experiencing. It is in these moments when we can feel our prayers are failing the most. After all, is not prayer the forming of words that create a conversation with God? Through those words, we express our adoration, our praise, even our requests. Otherwise, how will God know if he doesn't hear it from us?

There is this real and tangible nature to prayer. Even when we are alone and praying quietly to ourselves, we are still forming thoughts and sentences in our minds. We are assembling, somewhere in the recesses of our brains, a thoughtful and coherent presentation to the Lord. Until we cannot!

Communication Breakdown

When we find ourselves in moments when words fail, there is this potentially harmful notion that can invade our thoughts. If we cannot say it, then prayer is no longer a viable option. Therefore, we become truly helpless, especially at a moment when prayer is what we need most. If we cannot say it, it cannot find its way to God. Or so we think.

I have been called into situations where grief and trauma are hanging in a room like a thick fog. Attempts to move within that room feel like you are wading upstream against a waterfall. In those moments when words easily fail, you can even feel like your sense of empathy is disconnected, especially if you have not personally experienced what the others are going through. It is one thing for us to fall silent and struggle with what to say, but to hear silence in return can be quite distressing.

The silence of God has long been an area of struggle for spiritual pilgrims throughout the ages. Does God hear us? Does God even care? Those two questions seem to resonate most when God appears silent, and even more disturbing is when that silence occurs at our most dire time of need. Silence has a way of heightening our sense of feeling alone. It is one thing to want moments of silence for personal reflection, but it is another matter altogether when you need a voice of assurance and all you get is nothing, not even static.

To feel all alone in our prayers is truly a frightening proposition. To sense the silence of God, and at the same time be in a place where words fail, can leave us as if all hope has been abandoned. As troublesome as God's silence can be, an equally disturbing scenario is when the need is great, yet we are lost for words.

Thankfully, it is true that for the majority of us, those moments when we are truly lost for words are rare. What those difficult moments do bring to the forefront are the never-ending existential questions that have been part of our dilemma for centuries. What are we here for? Is there meaning to our existence and does suffering have purpose? At some point everyone, believer and unbeliever alike, has wrestled with those questions in one form or another.

Certainly, in times of struggle and suffering, our prayers are infused with the groaning of our hearts during difficult emotional seasons. The ever-present, yet elusive, answers to our questions in moments of hardship are common to everyone who has gone through such experiences.

Maybe it is my own self-reflecting nature when it comes to this topic of whether or not our lives have meaning and purpose that cause me to dwell on this subject. Times of difficulty do raise the existential questions more often, but they are always part of our human search for meaning, even though we live in a culture that seems to be more on a quest for happiness than anything with deeper human significance.

The Questions that Loom Large

As believers we grapple with an additional dimension to our lives that, frankly, unbelievers do not. We struggle with the whole matter of discerning God's will. That question rarely, if ever, darkens the minds of those unconcerned for the affairs of God, yet for believers, it is a continual tug of war.

I have rarely entered a semester where a student has not asked my opinion on what God's will may be for their lives. I have heard countless stories of students from every background and backstory imaginable who sensed a call upon their lives and then found themselves in college and seminary, while at the same time unsure of why they were there. The call is real, but specific details of what that call will look like is sketchy at best.

Being asked what God's will is for one's life is a little like christian fortune-telling. Especially when you barely know the person. Some may have the gift of spiritual discernment in such matters but for most of us, the ongoing question of God's will is a continual concern, regardless of how large or small the matter. We fret over the potential of missing God's will while at the same time wrestle with what it actually is.

In this short prelude, I have presented two different scenarios in our spiritual experience, which in many ways affects our prayer lives significantly. The first experience reflects those difficult moments when we have trouble formulating words for our prayers. The second is in the difficult moments when we have trouble discerning the will of God. Both of these may sound totally unrelated at first, but there is certainly a relationship between the two.

Both may very well leave us without clear or discernible answers or cause us to wrestle spiritually. Both certainly convey stark reminders of our human limitations. There are many times where we can be off the mark in our prayers, because we do not know or understand God well enough or are confused by what he may be doing in a present situation. We may even lack the confidence to pray, or struggle to comprehend the exact thing we need to be praying about in the first place.

Despite these challenges, Scripture gives us one of the more encouraging passages about prayer. It comes in Romans 8, a passage written by the apostle Paul, and considered by many to be the definitive chapter on what it means to be a Christian. To understand this chapter is to understand the profound implications of being a follower of Christ, with all the spiritual benefits that come with it. For our purposes here, we are looking at vss. 26–28:

> [26] And the Holy Spirit helps us in our weakness. For example, we don't know what God wants us to pray for. But the Holy Spirit prays for us with groanings that cannot be expressed in words.
> [27] And the Father who knows all hearts knows what the Spirit is saying, for the Spirit pleads for us believers in harmony with God's own will.
> [28] And we know that God causes everything to work together for the good of those who love God and are called according to his purpose for them. (Romans 8:26–28)

To say that these three verses hold a treasure trove of truth is somewhat of an understatement. The verse that garners the most attention is verse 28 with the stark reminder that everything that happens in our lives, God works out for good. For our purposes as it relates to prayer, the previous two verses are the focus of this segment.

In two short verses, Paul reassures believers in two areas of difficulty with respect to prayer—the times we are unsure of what to pray for and the times we are unsure of God's will. In other words, what do you do when life paralyzes you? For example, what about those moments when you are confronted with a major decision or need some direction regarding the future? When there are far more questions than there are answers, knowing how or what to pray for can be daunting. Leaning on the wisdom of others is always an option, and for the most part a good one, but Paul reminds us of another option when faced with paralyzing moments.

Supernatural Access

The key to this is the recognition of the Holy Spirit's role. One of the key distinctives of the Christian faith is the Holy Spirit. The Spirit plays a fundamental and important role in every believer's life, regardless of how much we understand or even acknowledge it. We have a powerful ally as believers, even in our prayers.

Let me give you a broad outline of the context of these verses as they are found in the greater teaching of Romans 8. Paul is talking about two ways of living. We can either live by the power of our human abilities with all their limitations and restrictions due to our fallen nature, or we can live by the power of the Holy Spirit. Paul is reminding believers that we live by supernatural empowerment because we are controlled by the Spirit. Further, Paul's reassurance is that there is a future glory for all believers and that nothing is able to separate us from God's love.

If you ever doubt the depth and the extent of God's love, Romans 8 is the text you need to run to every time such thoughts enter your mind, especially verses 35–39 which close out the chapter. Few poems, sonnets, or ballads of love come close to matching the eloquence of divine love expressed in these verses. They are a fitting conclusion to a chapter that is overflowing with doctrinal gold.

Communication Breakdown

What is striking about chapter 8 is Paul's full acknowledgement that our present life can be filled with difficulties and sufferings. In the section where Paul is communicating the depth of God's love (vss. 35–39), he reminds us that even if we experience "trouble or calamity, persecution, hunger, destitution, danger, or even the threat of death," we are still loved. For most, the experiences we go through are, to one degree or another, the measure of God's love. Yet here, Paul tells us this is not the appropriate rubric for understanding God's love. Regardless of what we are going through, we are never separated from God's love.

Those same difficulties are alluded to earlier in the chapter where Paul tells us the entire creation is groaning under the weight of death and decay. We, as believers, are groaning as well, even though we have the Holy Spirit as a foretaste of future glory, when we will be released from sin and suffering (vs. 23).

The Holy Spirit plays a key role in chapter 8, as Paul, time and again, places the Spirit in perspective for all who claim to be followers of Christ. Granted, for many, the Holy Spirit is somewhat of an enigma. Though there are vast libraries filled with theological treatises on the Spirit, it is a topic still shrouded in mystery for the average believer. We either treat the Spirit with respect, but with cautious avoidance, or we treat him as a wizard who performs whenever we need supernatural assistance.

Paul's teaching regarding the Spirit in this chapter is more pragmatic. Though we exist in a fallen world, one where the realities and effects of sin and death are all around us, we are never left to manage the struggles alone. This is not to sound obtuse or to throw around theological precepts in a cavalier or insensitive way, but for Paul, this has huge implications, especially in the more dire struggles we are experiencing.

The moments in which we are most at a loss, are the very moments the Spirit is there to intercede for us—the Spirit who knows our hearts and at the same time exists in perfect accord with God. Notice that nowhere is Paul stating we will get the answers we are looking for, or even a resolution to the problems that created the groaning in the first place. Paul does present in verse 28 the hope of your circumstances being used for good by God, but that is still a generic response to an almost countless number of possible scenarios.

In moments of trial and suffering, we long for answers or, at the very least, guidance. The major takeaway of Paul's teachings in this chapter is not about getting answers, but about the intercession of the Spirit. This intercession reminds us of his presence, comfort, and the necessity of aligning our spirit with the perfect will of God. Those are the priorities presented by Paul along with the reminder that regardless of the struggles we face, God will work it all out. In a pattern that we have seen time and again, the essence of prayer for us is more relational in its purpose than us getting everything we ask for. So, through the difficulties and uncertainties that exist as a part of life, we have an intercessor who effectively prays to the Father, when humanly speaking, it is most difficult to do so.

Our Ever-Present Help

In the Gospel of John, Jesus promises that he will send another comforter, namely the Parakletos, or otherwise known as the Holy Spirit (John 14:16, 26; 15:26; 16:7). Apart from the ministry of the Spirit in instructing and bringing to mind everything Jesus taught, the term that Jesus used for Spirit is filled with significance. If you were to survey the many translations we have in English there are a variety of terms that are used to convey the essence of Parakletos.

The word encompasses the many characteristics of the Spirit including counsellor, helper, comforter, intercessor, and encourager. It carries the idea of someone sent to assist with or advocate for the cause of another, whether in a judicial sense, or personal, beneficial sense. In the passages in John, the ministry of the Parakletos would help the disciples come to a deeper knowledge of divine truth, and equip them with the strength needed to face the persecution and trials they would undergo for the sake of the kingdom.

While many of us see prayer as a results-based enterprise, the results we often seek are different than the ones God would want for us. If you were to group the major categories that encompass the idea presented by Parakletos, they could be categorized as "ever helpful" and "ever present". Whenever we experience unanswered prayer, we somehow feel as if God exited the building, or at least ignored or denied the request. Rarely do we consider or accept other options as potential answers. In some cases, God allows us to experience the exact situation we are praying to avoid for reasons we cannot fully know or understand. Despite this, and against whatever we may be feeling, the Holy Spirit is always there and always ready to comfort and reassure us.

The Spirit expands our human capabilities and capacities. To experience divine enablement in our lives takes the indwelling power of the Holy Spirit. I would contend that to love as Jesus loved goes beyond our human limitations. This love takes divine empowerment. The same can be true for experiencing the trials and tribulations that life can throw our way and the ability to be able to ride out those storms—the same storms that would crush the spirit of others. Knowing and having the enablement and presence of the Holy Spirit allows us to withstand more than we thought possible.

Humanly speaking, we strive to try and fix people whenever we have the ability or power to do so. When someone is hurting, we long to take away their pain. We also know that there are times when we are unable to fix or alleviate the problem or pain. What we can do, though, in every case, is be there—to walk beside them, remind them that are not alone, and to demonstrate love and compassion. The same can be said for the ministry of the Holy Spirit as demonstrated in the teachings of Paul in this chapter. Yes, God is able to remove the problems and pains that initiate many of our prayers; he does not have the limitations that we do. But implied in the essential teachings of Scripture is a deeper reminder that when the answers are not evident or available, the presence and comfort of the Spirit are.

Another implication from the chapter we have been reviewing is the necessity of waiting upon the Lord. In a world where instant gratification is the norm, and a culture that promotes the need to have everything now, there is the counter message of patiently waiting. Waiting has a way of filtering out the excesses and allowing us to see what matters. It helps us to see that God's presence in our lives is not predicated by our service, our performance, or any privilege we feel we might have. It is awaiting God's timing and, in the process, growing in our communion with him.

Patience, long considered a virtue, is a natural and intrinsic part of the prayer discipline. Though it smacks against the urgency and spirit of impatience that is part of our culture, the profound nature of prayer is often found in the waiting, in the groaning, and in the longing that comes when heaven and earth meet. In those moments when we are unsure of what to say or what to do, we patiently wait on God, while the Spirit of God speaks on our behalf and carries us when we can no longer carry ourselves.

10

Focal Point

IF A STRANGER WAS to hear you pray, what would they learn about your faith? Would they learn anything about the character and nature of God, or even about his plan and purpose for humanity? Would they get a glimpse of Jesus Christ, or even a hint of the Gospel? Would our prayers convey a sense of awe and reverence, or would they sound more like another task in our never-ending list of demands that each of us face on a daily basis?

In the number of passages surveyed so far, we have witnessed within the essence of each prayer, an appeal to not only the character of God, but to his actions throughout history. Biblical prayers are far more than a series of requests for needs or wants, no matter how urgent or pressing. Even the Book of Psalms which is the definitive collection of prayers is not one-dimensional in its presentation.

The Psalms have long been recognized as one of the most read sections of the Bible. This is due to their intimate and relatable nature. We hear the deep passion, feelings, and demands that each Psalm writer communicates. We can wrestle with the Psalmist as they journey with God through the various experiences of life—a journey that many of us in our own sojourn of faith can clearly understand. Despite the deep personal nature of the Psalms, they are equally replete with deep reflections of the character and nature of God, as well as the many deeds that are directly attributed to him.

When we reflect on our own prayer lives, we often do not see it as a reflection of what we believe about God or as a demonstration of the depth of our faith. For the most part, our view of God and the way it affects our faith is almost always tied to the degree in which our prayers are answered. It is a type of cause-and-effect mentality as opposed to prayer being a spiritual quest. Is our faith consistent with our prayer life or is there a built-in hypocrisy that we are unaware of? Is God worthy of being worshipped if life remains difficult, and the answers to prayer limited?

Some may object to the notion of prayer being a witness of what we believe. It would appear to smack against the very purpose of prayer, at least from the way it is typically experienced on a popular level. Hopefully, having gone this far in our study, we are beginning to see a broader and more profound understanding of prayer, and its value in forming spiritual depth and maturity. This is not to minimize the aspect of prayer where we come to God with real needs—a refrain I need to continually stress. What we are arguing for here is a much deeper and more comprehensive understanding of prayer.

Coming Full Circle

Throughout his writings, the apostle Paul adds the content of his prayers as part of his message to the various churches he is writing. One such letter is his epistle to the Ephesians, written to the church that met in Ephesus, a city which at the time was the fourth largest in the Roman Empire. It was known for one of the seven wonders of the ancient world, the Temple of Artemis which was four times larger than the Parthenon in Athens. It was estimated to hold twenty-five thousand people, and was likely the largest Greek temple ever built.

Ephesus was considered the birthplace of Artemis, the goddess of fertility, nature, virginity, and the moon among others. It was the central hub for the worship of Artemis, and hosted a number of industries that supported the cult. It is to this city, steeped in the worship of a Greek deity, that Paul writes his letter to encourage a fledgling church which he founded on his second missionary journey. (Acts 18:19)

The cultural milieu of Ephesus is important to note, though it is not much different from what existed culturally in the world at the time. It is important because two of the societal norms that existed during the first century have become areas that challenge the church in our modern day: religious diversity and sexuality.

With respect to worship, the plethora of deities that existed in the first century are too numerous and too varied to list. A deity existed for practically every aspect and contingency of life, with attributed cultic practices and rituals related for each. It was not unusual for individual homes to have an altar dedicated to a patron god of the household. Cities and whole nations adopted patron deities and built temples to honor them.[1] Many of their ruins can still be seen today, and are part of the vacation itineraries of several of the tour groups in that part of the world. The cultic practices of the first century were an intrinsic part of life and deeply ingrained in society.

In terms of sexuality, the ancient world was rife with sexual sins, at least from a christian worldview. Homosexuality was common among the Greeks, and was even considered the noblest form of love. Practiced primarily by males between their early teens and early twenties, it was not considered inferior to heterosexual love. Even the gods were linked to all kinds of sexual immorality, and prostitution was a recognized institution that was part of many of the religious practices at certain temples.[2]

We are living in a culture that is looking more and more like the first century, especially in the areas of sexuality and religious diversity. For centuries we, in North America, have enjoyed a society based on christian values, but have quickly seen those values erode. This in no way is an argument for a nostalgic reversal of our present reality or an argument for christian nationalism. Far from

---

1. Ferguson, *Backgrounds of Early Christianity*, 166–72.
2. Ferguson, *Backgrounds of Early Christianity*, 63–64.

it. These points have been presented because they serve as vitally important backdrops for the prayer that will inform our study. If we are looking more like the first century, then this prayer by Paul in the book of Ephesians will help inform us on what should shape our prayers today, especially as they relate to the cultural issues that are dominating our society.

On a final note, few modern believers fully grasp what it meant for someone in the first century to convert to Christianity. The number and weightiness of cultural and societal norms they had to jettison was staggering. No longer could they participate in the cycle of rites and rituals that not only were part of their daily household routines, but also part of the city or town they lived in. Gone would be the acceptance of moral and ethical practices that were considered normal at the time, but were now to be avoided. It was leaving behind everything they knew and had grown comfortable with, and now venturing into a new relationship with an entirely new way of living and looking at the world.

A Striking Prayer for its Time

The prayer we are focusing on is found in the opening chapter of the book of Ephesians in vss.15–23. It is, in my estimation, a model prayer when burdened by the challenges that the church faces today. The prayer's opening verses are as follows:

> [15] Ever since I first heard of your strong faith in the Lord Jesus and your love for God's people everywhere,
>
> [16] I have not stopped thanking God for you. I pray for you constantly,[17] asking God, the glorious Father of our Lord Jesus Christ, to give you spiritual wisdom and insight so that you might grow in your knowledge of God.
>
> [18] I pray that your hearts will be flooded with light so that you can understand the confident hope he has given to those he called--his holy people who are his rich and glorious inheritance. (Ephesians 1:15–18)

Focal Point

Imagine if someone was to evoke this prayer for your church? Though the apostle Paul is credited for much of the doctrinal distinctives that defines Christianity, he had at his core, a pastoral heart. This is seen especially in the many prayers we find in his writings, and this one is no different.

In light of the cultural issues affecting the church at Ephesus, Paul's prayer is a lesson in focus. Though Paul acknowledges that the church is known for its strong faith and love for God's people, he prays for even more to be granted to the church. Some, in hearing this description of a church, would think they had arrived. What else would a church need beyond strong faith and Christlike love?

At the beginning of this chapter, we commented on how our prayers can communicate the character of God and the depth of our faith. In this prayer, Paul reminds us that knowledge of God is a never-ending and ever-growing experience. We simply cannot exhaust in this lifetime all we can know or experience of God. He is beyond our human comprehension, yet God has chosen to reveal himself through his Word, his son Jesus Christ, the Holy Spirit, and the church.

We presently live in a culture of more—more money, more cars, more house, more status, more, more, more. Even in the church, we see the effects of the "more culture"—more in attendance, more in offerings, more blessings, more salvations, more healing. But how many of us are praying for more of God? This is not to discredit the importance of growing churches or growth in key areas of our economy and livelihood, but this is meant as an encouragement to assess our priorities and focus. What we want more of is often an indication of our spiritual health and priorities.

For Paul, the challenges the church faces in whatever culture or time-period it exists, are secondary to what is critically important. If there is one thing that every church needs, it is more of God. Without a deep faith, the challenges of the culture can soon overwhelm and overtake us, to the extent that we can feel like we are losing, or that God is no longer in control. When cultural issues take precedence, we can quickly become churches that foster insulation from the outside world or an "us versus them" mentality. Neither of those postures help the church accomplish the task of the Great Commission as found in Matthew 28:18–20. Remember, the early church faced cultural challenges that we in North America are only beginning to experience, and yet they took the world by storm. There is nothing that the early church had that is not available to us. The same Holy Spirit that empowered them is the same Holy Spirit that empowers us today.

Christianity in the present is experiencing a season where deconstructing faith is in vogue. Faith deconstruction can be positive if it helps us to remove the shackles of, judgmentalism, legalism, racism, or christian nationalism. Removing these can create an environment for fostering an authentic Christlike faith—one that nurtures both truth and love. It is not good if it dismantles your faith altogether. When that happens, it becomes nothing more than spiritual suicide.

I am also intrigued by the way Paul delineates between the head and the heart in his prayer for the church in Ephesus. Without getting into the philosophical arguments of what constitutes the head versus the heart, especially in the first century, I am going to take a more pragmatic view. Paul prays that the Ephesians would experience more of God in everything they think ("to give you spiritual wisdom and insight so that you might grow in your knowledge of God"), and everything they feel ("that your hearts will be flooded with light so that you can understand the confident hope he has given to those he called").

Paul wanted the experience of the Ephesians to not be limited in any way. He wanted them to know God, not as an academic abstraction, or even as a purely experiential one, but holistically with their entire self. When it came to the spiritual well-being of fellow believers, Paul did not want any potential gaps. We will revisit this in the next chapter.

FOCAL POINT

A Potentially Neglected Piece

Embedded in these opening verses of Paul's prayer is another important element. We can acknowledge its presence while at the same time ignoring its importance. What we are alluding to is Paul's thankfulness to God for the church at Ephesus. Gratitude as an ongoing script in our prayers is like fertilizer to a plant. Biblical prayers are often reflections of gratitude. (See 1 Chron 16:8–36; Ps 30:12; 56:12; 75:1; 95:2; 136:2, 26; Dan 2:23; 6:10; Matt 15:36; Mark 14:23) In fact, gratitude is an important part of many of Paul's letters to the churches. (Rom 1:8; 1 Cor 1:4; 2 Cor 1:11; Eph 1:6; Phil 1:3; Col 1:3; 1 Thess 1:2, 13; 2 Thess 1:3; 1 Tim 2:1; 2 Tim 1:3; Philemon 4)

As a professor, one of the courses in my portfolio is spiritual disciplines. Considering the overwhelming biblical evidence for gratitude as a key component of prayer and worship, I am surprised by how little it is mentioned in the majority of resources that target the disciplines. What is it about gratitude that warrants so much biblical attention?

For one, gratitude is considered a "gateway emotion." It is a virtue that opens the door to many others. Similar to the experience of the Pevensie children opening the wardrobe to Narnia, gratitude is a portal to a whole new world.[3] Research studies have shown that gratitude tends to make people happier and less depressed.[4] A Forbes article recently stressed the real impact gratitude has on physical health, emotional well-being, motivation, engagement and belonging.[5]

If gratitude is proven to add positively to our overall joy and well-being, why are so many of us neglecting it as a regular part of our spiritual expression? We do tend to lean more into negativity and yet gratitude helps to reshape our attitudes and reactions to

---

3. Lewis, *Chronicles of Narnia*, chapter 1.

4. Brown and Wong, "How Gratitude Changes You and Your Brain," lines 8–9.

5. Brower, "Gratitude is Good: Why It's Important and How to Cultivate It," lines 4–6.

the trials of life in a more positive way. After all, the only thing we have any control of is our reaction to the things that come into our life. It is much easier to act like a Christian than it is to react like one. Gratitude helps us to reframe our experiences in a more positive way.

I think it is fair to say that God is continually at work, not only in the world around us but in us individually. That doesn't mean, though, that we easily recognize his work. We can become so caught up in the difficulties and challenges that we face on a regular basis that we can miss some significant things God is doing right in front of us. Gratitude has a way of forcing us to pause and take inventory.

It is one reason why many see the benefits of journaling. When it comes to gratitude, journaling is one way of being intentional in seeing the work of God in your life, and the many daily blessings we can be thankful for. A greater expression of gratitude builds better relationships, and helps foster a more positive outlook in others, because just as negativity breeds negativity, gratitude helps others see the grander picture.

To touch further on this point for a moment, another benefit that is bred by an attitude of gratitude is the way it expands the horizons of our appreciation. My own journey in developing a greater sense of gratitude is finding joy in the simpler things in life. This has led to seeing many things in my life that at one time were taken for granted as now being treasures that God has blessed me with. This may sound pedantic or trite at first, but it has the power to reshape your entire outlook.

Lastly, we are not talking about a gratitude that is superficial, feigned, or expressed for the sake of appeasement. It also does not ignore the difficulties that exist for each of us. It is, however, a deep acknowledgement of what and where God has blessed us, and then being cognizant and intentional in identifying those blessings and thanking God for them. As we have seen, the apostle Paul expressed gratefulness for every church he had the opportunity to interact with. For Paul, every faithful church became one more witness to the power of the Gospel, regardless of the challenges they were facing because of the surrounding culture.

More to Paul's Prayer

Paul continues his prayer to the Ephesians with some important reminders, both theologically and practically. The remainder of his opening prayer is as follows:

> [19] I also pray that you will understand the incredible greatness of God's power for us who believe him. This is the same mighty power [20] that raised Christ from the dead and seated him in the place of honor at God's right hand in the heavenly realms. [21] Now he is far above any ruler or authority or power or leader or anything else-- not only in this world but also in the world to come. [22] God has put all things under the authority of Christ and has made him head over all things for the benefit of the church. [23] And the church is his body; it is made full and complete by Christ, who fills all things everywhere with himself. (Ephesians 1:19–23)

In the closing section of this prayer, Paul continues his theme of wanting more for the church at Ephesus. He wants them to have more understanding of God's power, and of the centrality of Christ and his authority over everything. Power, for the apostle Paul, was not primarily the power of God to speak entire universes into existence. Power, for Paul, was the raising of Christ from the dead.

Christianity rises and falls on the resurrection of Jesus Christ. Paul states as much in 1 Corinthians 15:12–19. Here in Ephesians, Paul has begun his prayer by asking that the church receive more of God, while he concludes his prayer by reminding them of the truths they have come to believe.

Once again, we see embedded in these verses the pastoral heart of Paul, encouraging the believers in Ephesus to hold true to the tenets of the faith, regardless of the cultural onslaught that would have been coming from around them. The culture of the first century was filled with the cravings of power and empire. The military might of Rome had yet to meet its zenith, and the continual power play of city states for political supremacy was on-going. Power was for the elite and privileged, and for those who had the resources to secure it.

Despite the cultural realities, Paul stresses the true source of power and where true authority resides. It is not it the machinations of human desire and greed, but in the Christ who reigns with power and authority over his body, the church. We would do well to understand this dynamic for our own time with its own cultural challenges. Although the manifestations of power today are different than those of the first century, the destructive nature of power is not.

Rich Villodas in his book, *The Deeply Formed Life*, states that, " . . . prayer is a steadfast refusal to give ourselves over to either resignation or self-reliance. Resignation says things will never change. Self-reliance says we can change things on our own. The former is marked by despair, the latter by a futile confidence in our own efforts."[6]

This middle road between resignation and self-reliance is exactly where Paul places his prayer to the Ephesians, and why it is such an important model of prayer for our present times. If we are not careful, we can allow our present difficulties to cause us to despair, while for others, it can turn us into combatants of a battle we are ill-equipped to fight, because we have forgotten that ultimately, the battle belongs to the Lord.

Imagine if instead of praying that the culture around us would start acting like Christians, we instead pleaded that our churches would have more of Jesus? Maybe, just maybe, such a prayer is what will truly move the heart of God.

---

6. Villodas, *Deeply Formed Life*, 78.

11

OF KING AND KINGDOM

OUR PRAYERS SOUND MORE like hospital moans than a kingdom on the move. That may seem a bit harsh, but be honest about the predominance of prayers that you hear. I personally have always disliked the analogy of the church being a hospital. It may be true in terms of finding healing and restoration, but nowhere do I see that as being the place of permanent residence.

If we push the analogy of the hospital further, unless you work there, most of us are eager to leave as soon as we are able. If we see the church as nothing more than a hospital, then we should not be surprised when people leave after they have had their fix. It presents the church as a one-dimensional institution and says nothing of growing people deeper as disciples of Christ, or even of the ministry needs of serving and gathering as a community.

When Jesus said he would build his church he stated that nothing would be able to stop it, not even the powers of hell (Matthew 16:18). That to me is not a defensive or passive statement, but a statement of the church's ever-growing power over the darkness of the world. It is not a retreat and hide proposition, but a bold assertion to meet the challenges that the darkness brings, and be a light that delivers hope, restoration, and healing.

This is not to deny that there are times when the church needs to gather as a community to lament. When tragedy and human suffering have taken their toll, the gathering of a community to weep and mourn together is one of the most healing experiences we can bring to the world. Conversely, the church can also be where we celebrate the best that life has to offer and the blessings we receive daily from a gracious God.

At the outset of the book, we presented what we see as a shortcoming in the way that we understand prayer. For the most part, our prayers exist in two dimensions, the personal one and the community one. The personal one, or the first dimension, addresses the prayers that focus on the needs and requests for our personal benefit or gain. The community one, or the second dimension, speaks to the prayers that we evoke on behalf of others. Admittedly, these are simple categorizations, but nevertheless, they do frame the majority of what the discipline of prayer has become for many.

The two dimensions of prayer are nevertheless vitally important and continue to be a critical component of what makes prayer so valuable and so intrinsic to our spiritual development. How many of us can recount the number of answered prayers that literally made us stand back in awe of the way God answered. It left us hopeful, while at the same time grateful, for the merciful hand of God. How many of us have been overwhelmed by knowing the number of people who were praying for us that made us realize we are never alone, and that we were being loved and cared for?

I have witnessed difficult relationships resolve long standing conflicts simply because they were brought together by prayer. We have seen miracles of healing and impossible situations resolved, and with no other possible explanation other than the fact that people were praying. Few things invigorate our spiritual lives or the life of a community as the witnessing of answered prayer.

Please Do Not Miss It

The necessity of prayer and its centrality to the life of the believer cannot be denied or ignored. No one can dispute or refute it. What can be argued though is that, for the most part, we are missing a third dimension, what can be termed as the "kingdom dimension." The various biblical prayers that we have surveyed have pointed us to this additional element that was an intrinsic part of the scriptural petitions.

This kingdom dimension is the recognition of the sovereign hand of God and his plans and purposes in the midst of our own daily rhythms of life. It is an awareness and an acknowledgement of God's presence, and a surrender to his will as to the outcomes. It is seeing the church as much more than a community hub, but as Christ's continuing work of redemption and reconciliation to a world steeped in darkness.

It is also recognizing the character and nature of God in contrast to who we are. I am personally struck by some of the Old Testament prayers that did not blame God for the circumstances in which people found themselves. Nehemiah, for instance, acknowledged that the exile the nation of Israel was experiencing was due to the fact that they broke the covenant with God (Nehemiah 1:5–9; see also Daniel 9:4–11).

When framed in this manner, God does not become a bully or a harsh despot, but is instead seen as faithful to the positive and negative aspects of the covenant the nation had agreed upon. God was simply keeping his promises, even though it meant hardship, difficulty, and exile for the nation. In an age where God is blamed for virtually everything that is wrong in our world, the acknowledgement of personal culpability adds a sense of humility to our prayers.

What cannot be missed, though, is that just as there was a recognition of God acting in accordance with the negative aspects of the covenant, there were also the hopeful promises that came with obedience. Here is where the main prayer appeals would find their focus. Just as God had promised to punish in disobedience, he also stated that there would be restoration and hope beyond the judgement. As exile was coming to a close, the nation knew that a new dawn was just on the horizon.

The same can be said in our modern context. Our kingdom prayers must be prayers asking for God to act. The social and cultural ills that consume so much of our media attention are only truly resolved by divine intervention. We need people's hearts to be changed, not social policies to be altered. We need a renewing of people's minds and hearts turning to faith in Christ, not more constitutional laws. It is broadening the scope of our prayers to appeal for Christ's words in Matthew 6:10 to become reality, that we would indeed experience "heaven on earth."

This is not a call for christian nationalism, empire theology, or anything smacking of christian domination. It is nothing of the sort, but just as we surrender the outcome of our prayers to the Lord as we petition for personal and community needs, we can also surrender to God's will the larger matters of politics and state. It is not creating christian laws that will change the world, but people whose hearts have been changed by Christ who will. We can never expect anyone to make christian decisions if they do not have the indwelling of the Holy Spirit (1 Cor 2:14).

A final thought needs to be added here. As demonstrated in the prayers we have surveyed, the primary function of prayer is relational. In building our relational depth with God, we become more conformed to the image of his Son, Jesus Christ, and more aligned and in tune to what God is doing, not only in our own lives but in the lives of everyone around us. We begin to comprehend in more profound ways the deeper dynamics of love, grace, and truth, and how they can reshape the world that we live in. If we only use prayer in the two-dimensional framework of personal and community, our prayers can potentially become nothing more than spiritual scorecards. However, when we recognize and acknowledge the kingdom component of our prayers, they begin to grow exponentially.

Getting What We Need

Does the Bible give us a definitive answer as to what we can receive or expect when we pray? There are many instances of appeals to prayer, countless examples of prayer, and evidence of answers to prayer. The types of prayers and their answers are as varied as can be imagined. But are there any responses to our prayers that are not limited by context, and can be fair expectations of what can be received?

Two passages that do not appear to be limited by context are James 1:5–8 and Philippians 4:6–7. In other words, they seem to apply regardless of what it is you are praying for. Both these passages hold significant truths that will enrich our prayer lives immeasurably. Beginning with the James passage, it reads as follows:

> ⁵ If you need wisdom, ask our generous God, and he will give it to you. He will not rebuke you for asking. ⁶ But when you ask him, be sure that your faith is in God alone. Do not waver, for a person with divided loyalty is as unsettled as a wave of the sea that is blown and tossed by the wind. ⁷ Such people should not expect to receive anything from the Lord. ⁸ Their loyalty is divided between God and the world, and they are unstable in everything they do. (James 1:5–8)

If there is a prayer that God appears to always say yes to it is the prayer for wisdom. Biblical wisdom is far more than an accumulation of knowledge. Knowledge without the wisdom of proper application or use can be harmful, dangerous, and even cause collateral damage. We live in a world where knowledge is easily accessible, but wisdom is scarce.

Biblical wisdom is skillful living. This is the ability to not question everything, but to discern everything. There is a huge difference between the two. It is a life of integrity and maturity and knowing how the world works, while at the same time not being caught up in the trappings that leave others struggling under the weight of it. It is taking truth and integrating it into life with a humility that recognizes with reverence the hand of God in the created order.

The qualifier for attaining this wisdom is to do so with wholehearted faith, an important attribute in the book of James and seen early on in his teaching on prayer. James' appeal here is a call for sincerity of heart as one approaches God, who is generous in granting his wisdom. In fact, it makes total sense to me that wisdom from God would be one of the easiest prayers to be answered, considering the many decisions that inundate us on a regular basis. Wisdom is not based on feelings, but on knowing and trusting the power of God's promises.

Caution needs to be expressed here. My sense is a passage such as this is not meant for prayers asking for a parking spot at a busy mall. This is not meant to be applied in a frivolous way. Its implications are for those moments when it is beyond our capacity and foreknowledge, or when we are truly stumped on how to move forward. We can become so overwhelmed by information that we can spend much time analyzing the information that we become paralyzed by indecision. What is heartening, though, is that whenever we face uncertainty, we can ask God for wisdom in order to help clear away the fog and gain clarity and direction.

An Answer Beyond Understanding

There is another passage that is important to note as it pertains to answered prayer. It is found in the book of Philippians, written by the apostle Paul and it has some significant lessons for us today. The passage in question is from Philippians 4:6–7:

> [6] Don't worry about anything; instead, pray about everything. Tell God what you need, and thank him for all he has done. [7] Then you will experience God's peace, which exceeds anything we can understand. His peace will guard your hearts and minds as you live in Christ Jesus. (Philippians 4:6–7)

Over two thousand years ago, from the dark and cruel confines of a Roman prison, the man we know as the apostle Paul, wrote these words to the church in Philippi, Greece. Such words barely make sense when we consider the circumstances of its author. Cold, dark, and damp, the surroundings of a Roman prison would have pointed to anything other than peace.

Yet, what Paul writes has been etched on the hearts of believers for over two millennia because his message of peace stood in contrast to his experience of imprisonment. Rather than drown ourselves in constant worry, why not pray and give it all to God? If we have the capacity to worry, we naturally have the capacity to transform the energy spent on worrying into prayer. Oh, and do not forget, thank him for what he has done already because God has been there before. What is happening now is not new or foreign to him.

But it is the result Paul states that truly baffles me. When we pray and release it all to God, we experience . . . peace! Adding to the incredulity of it all is that it will be a peace that we cannot fully understand or comprehend. Why? Because from the outside, it will not make any sense. The inner peace that is being experienced will not make sense in light of the external storms that exist. While others are curling up into a fetal position, we are walking through the storm undeterred.

At the very heart of peace lies the conviction that we are trusting in someone or something beyond the present crisis—something that will exist and persist long after the crisis is gone. It is the primary reason that the apostle Paul can write of peace while experiencing the shackles of Roman imprisonment. What was a present hardship for him physically, was only temporary when considered in light of our faith in Christ, and of eternity.

Paul seems to anticipate the question many of us would ask. Where will I know this peace? His answer is one of the most comforting in all of Scripture. In our hearts and our minds, he writes. In other words, every feeling of anxiety and fear (heart), and every doubt and worry (mind), will be guarded. In the two areas where negative thoughts and negative feelings are generated, you will experience something so profound and unexplainable, except to say that we know it could only have come from God.

Unfortunately, we can read this passage as one that promises to fix or correct whatever we are asking from God. However, that is not what this passage teaches. The peace of God will be with you in the midst of our trials, whatever they may be. It is not a passage that promises God's removal of the storm, but of God's protection and presence in the midst of it.

It has been my experience that my head and my heart are rarely ever in sync. It is a never-ending tug of war. There are many things that I know intellectually that I don't always feel emotionally. For instance, I know I should not indulge in certain foods because they are not healthy, but my emotional response is another matter altogether. Have you ever heard the saying, "Love is blind?" That is when the heart takes over and any rational arguments are drowned out. It is reassuring to know that regardless of the discontinuity between my head and my heart, there is the potential to experience the protection of peace with both.

Prayer that Makes a Difference

For Paul, and for every believer since, the prospect of peace has always been a byproduct of faith in Christ—a divine enablement, and not the result of life's circumstances. There is a lot in life to be anxious about, and the list appears to grow each year as opposed to getting smaller. Paul, himself in a place that would warrant the need to worry, encourages us to pray and release it all to God, and in response, receive protection for our heart and mind.

As believers, we can think that our primary purpose is to serve God, or be a witness for God. As honorable as those may be, the primary purpose or mission is to simply be with him. It is the difference between thinking you work for God as opposed to being a child of God. The same can be true about changing our perception on the discipline of prayer. The real power of prayer is not what we get to ask God for, but what God is able to do in us that nothing in life can match.

Here is a list of summary statements that I hope you find helpful in understanding prayer in a new way and in a way that prompts you to pray with more attention to the kingdom purposes of God:

- Prayer is first and foremost a relational collaboration with the living God.

- Prayer is learning to release the outcome to God.

- Prayer reminds us of the reality of the spiritual world and the ongoing war that exists in the heavenlies.
- Prayer is recognizing that the battle belongs to God.
- Prayer is the most hopeful response to a hopeless situation.
- Prayer helps us manage our worries, fears and anxieties by releasing them to God.
- Prayer is acknowledging that we are not finished until God says we are finished.
- Prayer reminds us that we are never alone, and even when life paralyzes us, the Holy Spirit carries us along.
- Prayer reorients us to God's purposes for our lives.
- Prayer is the pathway to true wisdom and peace.
- Prayer is limitless, in its expression and practice. We are not limited by time of day or mode of communication.
- Prayer is the practice of aligning our hearts with God's heart.
- Prayer changes things, and is often the catalyst that God uses to do the miraculous.

We began this study acknowledging that for most of us, prayer exists within a two-dimensional framework, the first being the personal (help me, bless me, give me) and the second being the community dimension (help them, bless them, give them). We have argued for a third, the kingdom dimension, that acknowledges the plans and purposes of God's kingdom as part of the natural prayer rhythm for our lives.

This third dimension has been a part of every scriptural prayer that has been studied. From acknowledging the nature and character of God to recognizing his work in the world, this third dimension formed not only a part of each prayer, but a majority. Kingdom prayers are formed by petitions of "show me, mold me, teach me," and have at their core a heart for the will of God to be made known. If we have not been taking the biblical model seriously, and if we do not see it as a healthy template for our own experience of prayer, then we have been missing an important component—one that likely evokes the favor of God.

On a practical note, how many of us are praying for our local churches? Not for the people and the needs within that community, but praying that the church as a whole would be salt and light to its community. That each neighbor within a mile of the church would know that they are loved not only by God, but by the church. How many of us are praying for the unity of the church, not to alleviate conflict and differences, but to serve as a witness to the Gospel of Christ?

How many of us are even concerned for the church to succeed in its mission? Are we even troubled when we hear of the steady decline of church attendance, or do we pray for Jesus to "build his church?" Could it be that much of the decline we have seen in our society is a result of not being interested in the things that are important to God? Has the church lost its ability to touch the heart of God because it has lost its identity and purpose for existence in the first place?

To be clear, this book was not an exercise in discouraging you to not ask God for anything but was a simple reminder that prayer is much more than treating God as a slot machine. That comparison may be a bit over-stated, but if we are not careful, prayer becomes a one-dimensional enterprise, or at best, a two-dimensional enterprise. From a biblical framework, prayer is meant to be more than a conversation concerning needs. It is meant to be a deeper communion between frail souls and a perfect God.

The city that I lived in for many years has a street named Hope Street. What is interesting is the fact that it is a dead-end street. Now, I found it hard to believe that the people at City Hall in the city planning office did not see the irony of naming a dead-end street with the name "hope". Was it a disgruntled employee who named the street, or was it a way of making a statement about the city that was a kind of an inside joke? It has led to some comical conversations over the years and many questions as to what may have led to such an oversight in the first place.

Of King and Kingdom

Strange names for city roads aside, prayer is never a dead-end street. In fact, it is a wide-open road filled with hope. We may have forgotten some of its vital elements, but it is a spiritual exercise that God longs for us to nurture. My hope is that through this book, you will learn to pray with greater focus and clarity, not just as it relates to the many needs around you, but with a deeper awareness of the work of God's kingdom. Maybe in doing so, we not only have our hearts touched by God in transformative ways, but we also discover prayer that moves the heart of God.

Bibliography

Brower, Tracy. "Gratitude is Good: Why It's Important and How to Cultivate It." *Forbes*, January 3, 2021. https://www.forbes.com/sites/tracybrower/2021/01/03/gratitude-is-good-why-its-important-and-how-to-cultivate-it/?sh=3a5f5fa52a0f.

Brown, Joshua, and Joel Wong. "How Gratitude Changes You and Your Brain." *Greater Good Magazine*, June 6, 2017. https://greatergood.berkeley.edu/article/item/how_gratitude_changes_you_and_your_brain.

Ferguson, Everett. *Backgrounds of Early Christianity*. 2nd ed. Grand Rapids: Eerdmans, 1993.

Johnson, Darrell W. *The Glory of Preaching: Participating in God's Transformation of the World*. Downers Grove: IVP Academic, 2009.

Lewis, C. S. *The Chronicles of Narnia*. New York: HarperCollins, 2014.

Peterson, Eugene. *The Message Study Bible*. Colorado Springs, CO: NavPress, 2012.

Steinsalz, Aden. *The Essential Talmud*. New York: Basic Books, 1976.

Villodas, Rich. *The Deeply Formed Life: Five Transformative Values to Root Us in the Way of Jesus*. Colorado Springs, CO: Waterbrook, 2020.

Wright, N. T. "The Lord's Prayer as a Paradigm for Christian Prayer." In *Into God's Presence*, edited by R. L. Longenecker. Grand Rapids: Eerdmans, 2001.

Manufactured by Amazon.ca
Bolton, ON